OLD
HUNDREDTH

OLD HUNDREDTH

BY JOHN GOULD

Illustrations by F. Wenderoth Saunders

W · W · NORTON & COMPANY
NEW YORK   LONDON

The text of this book is composed in Palatino.
Composition and manufacturing by The Maple-Vail Book Manufacturing
Group.

First Edition

Library of Congress Cataloging-in-Publication Data
Gould, John, 1908–
Old hundredth.
I. Title. Essays about life in Maine.
PS3513.085204   1987   811'.52   86–23844

ISBN 0-393-02444-X

W. W. Norton & Company, Inc., 500 Fifth Avenue, New York, N.Y. 10110
W. W. Norton & Company Ltd., 37 Great Russell Street, London WC1B 3NU

1 2 3 4 5 6 7 8 9 0

This book is for my mother
on her 100th birthday
anniversary

Hilda D. J. Gould

She was born at Millview,
near Vernon River, Prince
Edward Island, Canada, on
December 14, 1886

* * * * *

Toilichte cendamh, Mathair!

Contents

CONTENTS

Peter Partout's Page

Dear Mr. Editor: Not long ago Mrs. Gould told me that
she didn't mind the thought of aging, but it was
disconcerting to realize she has four children who are all
senior citizens.

(Signed) Peter Partout

Peppermint Corner

Old Hundredth

Praise God, from whom all blessings flow;
Praise Him, all creatures here below;
Praise Him above, ye heav'nly host;
Praise Father, Son, and Holy Ghost.
                    Amen.

                    —Thomas Ken, 1709
                    Bishop of Bath and Wells

OLD
HUNDREDTH

The Difference

They seem so happy about it. "Goodbye, goodbye," they say, "we'll see you next spring!" Then they fly south. They seem gleeful about being listed in our annual town report as "non-resident taxpayers," and in spite of that are fine people and a good addition to our down-Maine community. Summertime friends, they remain nonresident, and also as summer complaints, rusticators, cottagers, seasonal visitors, and even dogfish. (The dogfish, a small shark, arrives in our waters at approximately the same time, and ruins the haddock fishing.) But not tourist—the tourist comes and goes and stops overnight, and the tourists tell us they can buy gasoline in Massachusetts cheaper than they can in Maine. (That's the place to buy it!) Our summer folks own their places here, and some had grandfathers who owned the same places. They support our library and ambulance; they take an interest. But, Labor Day is the difference, and off they go to pass the winter waiting for spring. They don't mean *spring;* they know little about a Maine spring.

Our Maine spring is elusive, and comes grudgingly between February and the Fourth of July, more or less, and not much at a time. I consider that spring is on the way when my mailman comes with his automobile window open and can reach mail into my RFD box without his mittens on. He'll broach the subject of a warming trend by saying, "Got anything plarnted yet?" He's in the habit of saying words like plarnted to amuse the summer people, and by asking that question he doesn't expect me to give him a crop report. I do have some petunias sprouted, and some celery and some onions, but it's too early for other things. He's just calling attention to the change in the weather which, at this time, has mellowed February. Maine will often have a few pleasant days along about Washington's birthday (O.S.), but it's too early to cheer. Things tighten up again, and then we have the hic-labor-est of struggling up the nigh side of March Hill. Get over the hump of March Hill, and things are downgrade.

But many's the winter that we get our sharpest nights and our deepest snow after the calendar shows the theoretical arrival of equinoctial spring. Oh, yes—there was a May when the orchards were in full bloom and the glad pomological perfumery was thick upon the land, and we woke the next morning to a foot of snow. That took the joy out of everything, and ruined the apple crop. But if things run any kind of a normal course, we'll have our little Washington's birthday hiatus, and nothing else of promise until mud season. Mud season doesn't mean so much since we got most of our roads paved, but there is still plenty of squish to track in on clean floors. In an old-time mud season the mailman would churn through, the chains on his rear wheels tossing goo into the treetops, and he'd say, "May not make it the next few days!" And we wouldn't expect him to. On that post office in New York where it mentions snow and rain and gloom of night, it doesn't say a word about Maine mud season. But paved roads have lessened the inconveniences, and mud season today is mostly a way to measure the time. Nobody who's gone for the season would know how we look upon mud season as a pleasant harbinger. It's frost-out time.

Right after mud season we have one of the best days of the year. It's when the sun dries up a spot on the south side of the barn, and we can let the hens out to frisk and frolic. Shut up all winter, they've forgotten what bare ground is. Watching the hens come out is great fun. When they find the door open, they naturally suppose it's ajar by mistake, so they have a big discussion

amongst themselves, as if sharing a big secret, and they take turns looking out to see if anybody has noticed the open door except them. But biddies have not been liberated, so they show only their heads until the rooster has investigated. He looks out, makes a speech outlining purposes and policy, and finally hops through the door to gaze about and make sure the coast is clear. He will demonstrate that all is well with a great flopping of wings, a recitation, and a crow that nearly knocks him over backwards. At this, his wives come streaming out and there is universal approval of this renewal of the seasons. Along in the afternoon the sun will fall behind the barn and this warm spot will cool off, leaving the birds bewildered. But a handful of corn will entice them back through the open door, and it may be some time yet before they'll be let out again. Could have snow before morning.

I guess the surest sign that spring has returned to Maine is the first woodchuck. Any spurious notion that a woodchuck and Candlemas Day coincide is as un-Maine as bananas growing in Baxter State Park. No honest Maine woodchuck will appear before the middle of May, and usually nearer to June. In February there is nothing for a Maine woodchuck to eat, and the only reason one comes out in May is to eat. He won't care if he sees his shadow or not. He wants green grass, and green peas. Having plarnted his traditional green peas on the 19th of April, a Maine gardener is not going to watch for woodchucks as harbingers of spring. He doesn't keep the .22 rifle handy for shooting shadows. Then, after the first woodchuck, swallows are all right. But not bluebirds. Bluebirds are liars. A swallow flirts and dips and tweeters, and is reliable, but the first bluebird always gets frost-bite and goes back to Guatemala for another three weeks.

But spring always does come. It's good to see a boy running all over town to show the trout he caught—the ice has gone from the pond! Then we have the cleansing flight of the bees. They've been in the hives since the goldenrod waned, and now with a warm forenoon they burst into the air and, relieving their pent-up situations, horribly daub the laundries on the lines. Then the bluebirds come again, this time to stay, and they have a big fight over bluebird boxes with the tree swallows. The tree swallows always win. Next is a yellowhammer, dipping through the orchard, and then the bees find the first dandelions and come to the landing boards with yellow legs. Now some other things can be plarnted in the garden, and spring seems to have arrived with its promise of summer. Promise, too, of July and August after summer in Maine is spent, and goldenrod shows again in the fields and along the roads. Goldenrod, in turn, promises frost in just six weeks, and by that time the summer-complaints will be gone again.

"See you in the spring!" Indeed. Spring, in Maine, is not exactly a date on the calendar. It comes when it gets good and ready, and before we see any summer folks we'll have another blizzard.

Close to Camp

Being surrounded pretty much by summer people, I get—maybe twenty times a season—the question, "And do you stay here all winter?" There's a smirk goes with it, as if nobody in his right mind would stay in Maine all winter. But I do stay here. In a way, I'm grateful for winter, because all the summer people are in Florida so they can send us postcards that say—as if rubber stamped—"Delightful here and we keep thinking how you're shoveling all that white stuff!" Today, as I take pen in hand to commence, is Friday, the 13th of December, 1985. That's a bad day to start anything. The morning was frosty but not cold—eighteen by Mr. Fahrenheit—and I surmise the forecast of snow is correct. Storms along our Maine coast shape up on a slack tide, so I think the first flakes will appear about noon. We had a new moon yesterday, so we're getting those high tides. Almost twelve feet here at Back River, so maybe this promise of snow will bring more than a flirt. Tides like these have been known to foment a foot or so of that "white stuff." There's a fringe of ice around the shore of Back River—we can see it from the sinkshelf window—and this is good because it hides all the white plastic oil bottles the tides have washed up. Boat people add oil to their engines and then heave the bottles into the drink. Why hasn't somebody made a green or brown oil bottle so it will blend with the rockweed, goose greens, and sea lavender?

Thinking a Friday the Thirteenth might need mollifying, I propitiated right after breakfast by lifting some lamb chops for supper from the freezer. And a package of green peas. There's some squash already cooked, and we'll bake some Green Mountain potatoes. Apple pie made with Northern Spy apples. So an unlucky day should be rendered docile, and I say let it snow.

Did I ever tell you about the time Mamie Gordon went to pass a winter with her daughter in Florida?

The daughter had a trailer in a trailer park, and she thought it would be nice if Mamie came down to get away from all that ice and snow of a rugged Maine winter. Mamie decided that would be a sound plan! That past summer, Mamie had been cook at a lumbercamp on Spotted Mountain, about twelve miles from town. The camp closed down operations back in September, and Mamie had stayed on alone until time to go to Floridy. She had plenty of firewood and grub, and as a veteran of many winters alone in the Maine woods it was nothing for her to amuse herself. Then the deer hunting season opened, and that area gets hunted for fair. Mamie could look from her camp the whole length of Kennebago Lake, with mountains on both sides and beyond, so every time a rifle went off the echoes would resound and Mamie liked to figure out what happened. Well, there'd be a shot from down by the Big Sag, and Mamie would say, "He got that one!" A single shot usually means success,

but if a hunter empties his magazine—bang-bang-bang-bang—
it's a good guess he missed with the first shot and then threw
some extra bullets in high hopes. Bombarding a "flag" makes
poor eating—the flag is the flip of the white-tailed deer's white
tail as he says goodbye and bounds out of sight over a blow-
down and mocks your marksmanship. Then Mamie would hear
a shot in Blanchard Swamp, and the untouched deer would
run up over the beech ridge with everybody in the party taking
a crack as it went by. The echoes would amplify this volley into
a barrage like a replay of the Civil War and Mamie would
chuckle, because by now the deer was well over into Lang-
town. So as the hunting season waned, Mamie packed up and
started for Floridy.

She got a Triangle Bus at Rangeley, and changed to a Greyhound at Lewiston—Loyst'n, that is. The Greyhound took her
nonstop to Florida and let her down right at her daughter's
doorstep. Quick as that. Mamie and her daughter embraced,
and before Mamie took off her hat and co't she sat in a chair
to relax from her trip. She had a glass of clear sauce that her
daughter thought might help her relax, and it sure tasted some
old goo-ood after that bus trip! Just then a gun went off right
under the window where Mamie was relaxing. She jumped
about out of her skin and spilled her sauce all down her front.
"Jeez-to-Mighty!" she shouted. "They sure as hell hunt in close
to camp down here!"

Yes. The neighbor in the next trailer, six feet away, had found
a rattlesnake under his steps and a policeman had come to shoot
the snake with his revolver. Mamie had never seen a rattlesnake, and the sight of this one tarnished her opinion of Florida.

So it's an expression, sort of, and in the winter we folks hunt
in close to camp, to the stove, and to the cribbage board. The
seed catalogs will come to cheer us with bright pictures and
similar hopes of tomatoes and cucumbers, and every morning
we have to make crucial decisions about what we'll lift from
the freezer to sustain our humdrum existence. We do socialize

some, and in recent winters our circle of socializers has widened—we now have some one-time summer people who came first to vacation but have retired, winterized, and embraced the privileges and duties of Maine natives. Now, they, too, get asked if they stay in Maine all winter. I saw one of them in the post office the other day. He stomped snow off his boots and bought stamps so he could mail postcards to people down in Floridy.

He Was Nine

Tooling my pickup truck towards the city on a bright summer afternoon, I came upon a bunch of people in the road and a fire engine. A search party was about to take off into the woods to find a lost child, and a state policeman was giving instructions. The vast forest in which this search would take place ran to at least ten acres and had streets on all four sides, so I said it looked to me as if things were well in hand and I pushed on about my errand. The day was comfortable, and I just hoped the black flies wouldn't chew the tyke to death before he was found. I drove on thinking about our two youngsters, who never got lost in the woods. There was a story in the newspaper the next day that the lad was found in good shape and in quick time, and there was a picture of him restored to the arms of his happy mother. He was nine.

The year that our lad was nine in June he announced, in December, that he would undertake the Christmas tree excursion by himself. Going for Christmas greens is traditional Maine winter adventure, and I'd been looking forward to going again with the lad in our usual way. Pack a lunch and spend most of a Saturday. Since he'd been going to school, winter Saturdays in the woods took on an importance in addition to being fun. I thought his school week was strenuous beyond the reasonable demands of an education. First, there was the long bus ride to town and the long ride home—enough to weary anybody before a book was opened. Then, he had to take part in an exhausting physical exercise program—I had become lenient about the small chores we asked him to do at home because his school athletics kept him pooped. So I'd feed his chickies for him, throw down hay for his calf, bring in his firewood, and leave him that much more time for his homework. On the Saturday, I'd get him off into the greenwood where he could forget about school and build up his strength for the next week.

But this next Saturday, a couple of weeks before Christmas, was to be his first alone in our woods. Seems he had volunteered to get a tree for his schoolroom, and then he'd taken orders for a half dozen from village people. Also, he'd need one for our living room. Then some greens for a few wreaths. He elaborated on his plans all week, and along about Thursday his sister Kathryn pointed out that the number of doughnuts he was planning to take would prove sadly insufficient. Kathy, then, was five. Thus she adroitly worked herself into the context, and without his knowing just how or when the lunch was planned big enough for two. Instead of "I" he was now saying "we," and I was glad to notice he had no misgivings about a distaff intrusion into his affairs. And Kathy was nigh as woodswise as he was. Both had helped with the springtime maple syrup work, had gone with me to haul wood, had helped fetch the cows from pasture, and I'd had them both along the brook trying for trout. Then we'd had family picnics. I'd told them how to keep from being lost, and how to find themselves if they did get lost. Nothing to panic about, I said. "There's nothing in the Maine woods can hurt you except, maybe, yourself." Thing to do is hunker down and think things over. Folks who get lost and regret it are the ones that run around in circles, and if you run in circles you're hard to find. One day I lost him on purpose, and a half hour later I came back to find him pounding a pine with a stick—that's to keep him busy so he'll be warm, and to make a noise without shouting himself hoarse. He looked at me when I walked up and said, "I sat down to think, and I thought you did that on purpose!"

So that Saturday we, the parents, stood by the kitchen window and watched the two set out on the Christmas greens adventure. He had his own boy's ax and Kathy was pulling the little red sled with the lunch tied on. The snow wasn't all that deep, but their legs were short. They didn't move fast as they went up through the fields and into the pasture, towards the woods. We turned from the window then, about other things, and at noon we sat quiet at the kitchen table—wondering what was going on in the family forest.

Mother spotted them about half past two as they came back into sight. Kathy was on the sled and the lad was pulling the string. Now, leaving the pasture, they had a downhill cant, and the sled ran ahead by itself. They weren't long in gaining the house, and Kathy came in to shuck her boots and stick her feet in the oven. She fell asleep right there, but not until she told us the day had failed to produce any woofs. The lad told us he tried to explain to her that we don't have any woofs in the Maine woods, which is true, but she wanted to see a woof and was disappointed. If Uncle Remus has woofs, there must be woofs. Then she fell asleep.

The lad said they had lunched by the spring, after he had whacked some hemlock branches to lay down like a blanket on the snow. He got the cups filled and balanced them on a stump. Then they had their lunch. After that, they cut some fir boughs, and hunted for good Christmas trees. Kathy was still nodding by the stove, and while I pulled on some boots and my mackinaw the lad went to start the tractor for me and bring it to the dooryard. The trees, he said, were all by the woods road, and the pile of boughs for wreaths by the spring. I noticed how red his cheeks were, and as I drove off to get our Christmas greens he went to join Kathy at the stove.

I found everything just as he said. The trees were lined up with their butts towards the woods road, and the tips for the wreaths by the spring. I found half a doughnut stuck into the crotch of a small maple, with a chickadee perched on it, and I saw the broken limbs on a birch—to mark the place where they left the road to go amongst the trees.

These were the things I thought about that summer afternoon as I tooled my pickup truck into the city on an errand. It was a pleasant summer day, and I imagine the black flies did get to that youngster before the search party did. Maybe the experience would teach him the wisdom of getting lost in cooler weather. We see very few black flies during December.

Between and Neither

E very fall, when summer is long gone, there falls a day that is much like other fall days, except that it isn't the same. It's hard to say why it's different, but we sense it is. It's a day that doesn't feel fallish, but suggests winter—in between and neither. There was one year it came the day before Thanksgiving, and it threw our plans askew.

I wouldn't call the day a "breeder," which is a Mainer's term for a fine day, any time of year, that soothes and comforts the unwary citizen with promise of a bright tomorrow, but which is really "making up" a foul day. Breeders go with the continuing rote of weather that goes with living all that close to Nova Scotia, where they never have a good day. In Nova Scotia they have only stormy days and breeders, a consequence of unpropitious exposure to North Atlantic oddities. So we know what breeders are, and this fallish day I speak of is not a breeder. It's a day that closes the account book of summer and changes everything over to a winter schedule. The weather people, now posing as meteorologists, don't recognize this day for what it is and offer portents and guesses fit for any other day. They don't take notice, to begin with, of the kind of frost that prevails just before sunup. Maybe they don't go to work before sunup, although in a Maine November the sun doesn't appear until going on seven, or what we call mid-forenoon. Come to look out the kitchen window while running water for the coffee, a witness will see pretty much the same pre-dawn white frost that has been going on since about October, but this morning there is a new cast to it. It has a new beauty, as if poised to make everybody glad. Then the sun pokes up and the frost changes from gray-white to white, then glister-white to pink, and from pink to a rousing ruby red that just about pushes the witness back from the window. The whole kitchen is rosy, and this gives a frivolous tinge to the oatmeal and frying eggs and brown-hashing potatoes. Pink oatmeal? For a half hour or so the wonderful world is a bower of roses. The unpainted old henhouse with the yank in its ridgepole becomes an enchanted fairyland cottage for elves and Goldilockses. As the sun creeps higher, it melts the snow on the henhouse roof, and the eaves drip with magic crimson sugarplums—and then the rosy dawn is over and the henhouse is just an old henhouse again with a yank in its ridgepole. The dawn-fire was fleeting, limited to once a year—and now we know this is the day that ends our fall.

The air is calm, and it will stay calm all day. Smoke from chimneys goes straight up, and the windvane hasn't moved from the southwest where it was at sunset last night when the breeze calmed for the evening. Today the air will stir again shortly, and it will turn the vane to east and northeast—towards Nova Scotia. But so far there is no breeze, and this is a morning when noises come from afar and sound close at hand. The down-state freight train, whistling for Farrar's crossing fourteen miles away, might be right under the window. The mill whistle, at the village, comes right into the house now, and most mornings we don't hear it. Roosters for miles around are answering one another. A bluejay in the upper field screams and seems to be on the doorstep. On a morning like this the distant fox going home will snarl at some fancied insult and wake the farm dog under the stove. I saw a doe on such a morning pass through the ruby frost, lifting hooves high as if leery about disturbing the scenery, and taking her time. On any other morning she would pass in a flash, clearing the pasture fence by ten good feet.

But what the day does and how it feels are incidental to the message it brings—this is the day to make ready for winter. It may snow before evening—and a prudent forecaster will add that it may not. But now is the last chance to make the rounds and gather in whatever is lying about—tools, apple baskets, playthings, this and that. Look everything over to be sure it's ready for winter. There was one year we had a dry fall and bad woods fires, so I'd left the orchard spray tank filled with water and ready—a fair fire engine if we needed it. I had to drain it, grease it, and back it under the storage shed. So now I took down the play swing from the maple on the lawn. I looked for jugs and pails that might be left with water in them. This is the day.

And this time it changed some of our Thanksgiving planning. I didn't get to shine up my wooden bowl of apples, and I didn't get to bring the mincemeat up from down cellar. I didn't get to bring up the apples for the pies, and when somebody else went for them he got the wrong kind. The kitchen routine was accordingly upset, and somebody forgot to tell me the right time to go to the bus stop and meet our guests from away. I was up fastening the big hay doors in the barn gable, and with only ten minutes' warning I got to the bus stop and found our friends sitting on their suitcases on the sidewalk. They asked what kept me, but I didn't go into details about how this was the day to make ready for winter.

After my careful readying, it would have been good to wake up on Thanksgiving and find a new fall of snow had hidden the browns of a dreary fall, but this time the day that foretold winter was a mite premature. Maine is sometimes like that. We didn't get snow for two weeks. But there's nothing wrong with Thanksgiving, and if the day disports like one in August I'll take it. I'm thankful I got the dooryard readied—it could have snowed!

Looking Good

An ancient uncle of the family who remained a bachelor until he died in his eighties always popped his apple seed first. It was kind of comical. I suspected he had some knack about picking the right seed, because he knew a great many odd and assorted things otherwise, and could well have made a study of the thermal capacities of a cookstove and the explosive characteristics of various pomological embryonics. He didn't talk like that often, but he could. Anyway, he used to smile and say that his seed popped first because he had led a clean life, kept reasonable hours, and always lifted his hat all the way off when he greeted a lady. He'd sit there, and we'd all sit there, waiting to see whose seed popped first, and Uncle always had a smug smile as if he knew very well that his seed would win. Which it did, and then we'd laugh, because the one whose seed pops first is going to be the first one to get married.

It's really not all that simple. We forget too readily that small and inconsequential things that mean so much in memory were parts of larger adventures, and while people could very well sit around a hot stove nowadays and pop apple seeds, it wouldn't be the same. May we agree that things have changed?

But it helped with winter evenings. If you've never popped

apple seeds and wish to know about it, the first thing to do is buy an ax. Then you need a woodlot and a brisk winter day, without too much snow on the ground, and a desire to live in a warm house next—not this, but next—winter. Easter is the dividing day, and while it is a movable date, it is the annual gauge for getting next winter's wood under cover. Under cover— that's tiered or stacked in the shed, where it will have all the coming summer to dry and be ready for the fires that will cheer the family 'twixt next freeze-up and thaw. Whether Easter came early or late, the prudent Mainer had his firewood cut, hauled, yarded, fitted, and stacked, and would brag that he was finished by Easter. The only way to answer him was, "Me, too!"

In the days of axes and bucksaws, two men working together could cut more wood in a day than three men working alone, and now with a chainsaw one man is aplenty. So have the other aspects changed, and where is the kitchen with a woodstove, a woodbox, and a family disposed to pop apple seeds? The *homeyness* of the old winter kitchen will never come again. The woodbox was the best seat in the kitchen, and that's where our octogenarian uncle perched. Some evenings he would nod from the heat of the stove so nearby and fall asleep, and then he would rouse, excuse himself, and go to bed. When that happened, somebody else would get the woodbox. But on nights when dry beans were picked over, the woodbox was too far away; everybody had to sit at the big table. It took a barrel or two of beans to see a family through, and after they were threshed and winnowed they had to be picked free of pebbles, sticks, culls, and whatever else shouldn't go in the pot. Father would dump a peck of beans in the center of the table, and one by one every bean was looked at. On beanless evenings Mother might read aloud from *The Youth's Companion*. The little ones would recite from the primers, otherwise, and Father always had *The New England Homestead*. But whatever went on, there would be a lull for fun, and like as not the apple seeds would get popped.

You needed an orchard. Not one of these present-day apple

factories that turn out macks and cortlands and delicious and never a good apple. What you need is an old family orchard that ran to Baldwins and Spies, and Blue Pearmains and Bell-flowers, and Nodheads and Hubbartston Nonesuch, and Golden Russets and Black Oxfords. Winter varieties that mellowed in the dark cellar and came along, kind by kind, with the calendar. Spies would "come in" before Christmas, but Black Oxfords would stay firm until June. The way it worked with us, Uncle would be on the woodbox and close enough to the stove to work the popcorn popper. While he was at that, a pan of apples would be brought up, cool and snappy from the cellar. Then butter and salt would drench the popcorn, and things were looking good. Oh—we grew our own popcorn, and shelled it off the cobs by rubbing two cobs together over a bowl. Contrary to erroneous notions about what old-timers did with spent corncobs, the truth is that ours were saved to make smoke when we cured hams and bacon. After due attention to popcorn and apples, everybody would have his apple seed picked out and ready.

You didn't just take any old seed. When you got down to the core you'd study the seeds to find the fullest. Some seeds wouldn't fill out. You wanted a good brown seed that looked fat and contented. And when everybody was ready, including Uncle, we'd reach and lay our seeds on the hot cover of the kitchen range. Interesting how the seeds will skip and dance about on the hot cover. They begin to steam up inside, and most of them will turn over. Now and then an odd one will teeter-totter all around the top of the stove. But one of them will be the first to pop, not unlike a kernel of popcorn, and usually it jumps off the stove to be lost in the dark corners of the kitchen. A sure sign of early matrimony. We had a cat who was never ready for the first pop, and would rouse and climb up the wall. Couldn't get used to it. Then Uncle would say, "Clean living!" and smile, and remark that perhaps it was time to go look for a girlfriend. With Uncle playing, we had to fore-tell weddings by the second pop.

It can still be fun. Just the other night we had a young lady visiting, and she saw her first apple seed pop on the top of our woodstove. She's eight. She clapped her hands at the happy promise of an early wedding, and we wished her every joy. I had an apple seed on the stove at the same time, and mine didn't pop at all. I never knew Uncle's secret.

From the Bunghole

After the summer people leave and Maine is restored to righteousness, it's a fine idea to press a barrel of cider. This adds a great charm to a Maine winter, never discernible from, say, Myrtle Beach, offers meantime amusement, and gives the promise of an interesting consequence along about February. By February a well-attended barrel of October's sweet cider will have an interesting piquancy that must not be undervalued, and a sturdy reliability which is as good as money in the bank. The prudent householder doesn't need to wait until February, however, because a prudent householder will always have some left over from previous Februaries, and prudence is a matter of constant supply. I have always explained to summer people, when I treat them in July and August to a honk from my constant supply, that I do not make cider. Cider is made by the Almighty, who remains our Best Authority. He devised the process in Genesis and it altereth not. The process is designed to make vinegar, which is good on pickles and sauerkraut and fiddlehead greens, and February cider is merely a way station. Sweet in October, cider acquires enzymes, calories, isotopes, carbohydrates, and trace elements of seventy-eight other commodities by February, which aid both digestion and erudition if applied to the right places. Cider thus sanctified will remain man's second-best friend indefinitely if respectfully attended, but when left to God's immutable plan it will begin to acetify and take on the talents so useful to cucumbers and fiddleheads. Vinegar, we must concede with pious respect, is God's purpose, but in His wisdom He has left us an ample meantime which we are free to embrace. But let us not linger on thoughts of February dalliance, but return to October, when the Almighty begins:

It was on an October day that I said to the youngsters, "When you're to the store Saturday, have Mommie pick up a package of straws."

"Straws?"

"Eyah—like the ones to suck a sody."

"What do you want straws for?"

"Can't you jokers ever do anything you're asked to do without asking questions about it? Why don't you just see that Mom gets some straws and take it for granted I know what I'm doing?"

"Sure! Okay! But why do you want some straws?"

Mommie, who has lived with me a bit longer than the children have, may have surmised, but she didn't ask any questions. For a few days we had domestic wonder about straws. Then, on the right Saturday I hove my grainbags of apples into the pickup truck, rolled up a sixty-gallon barrel, set in a dozen jugs, found the children, and off we went to Mr. Mosho's cider mill up on the No-Name Pond road. Mr. Mosho's cider mill was adjacent to and part of a larger operation that produced an esteemed product known as Moosehead Applejack. He and God would start off together, but when God was finished Mr. Mosho added one more step and distilled his hard cider into a multidimensional brandy that made both a beverage and an explosive. But first he had to press apples and lay away sweet cider. It was useful to him to open his place to the public and press apples for everybody who came along.

That's why I set a dozen jugs into the pickup. You see, if you brought too few apples and the juice didn't fill your barrel,

Mr. Mosho would sell you enough to fill. But if you brought too many apples and had some juice left over, Mr. Mosho would keep it and he didn't pay you anything. In this way, during a pressing season, Mr. Mosho acquired considerable cider that didn't cost him a cent, and his applejack ledger kept him happy. So I did have some extra cider that day, and we ran it off in my jugs and thus saved it from a horrible fate at the hands of Mr. Mosho. "You got a good juice," he said, and he charged me $3.50.

It was a good juice. I smile to myself every fall when I drive by these wayside stands and see the little signs that say, "McIntosh Red Cider." For some reason the McIntosh Red apple has achieved fame and popularity far beyond its true worth, although the skins can be cut up into serviceable shoestrings. Cider made from McIntosh Reds alone is by no means the best. The best is made from a blend of several apples, none of which is McIntosh. Russets should always be used, and so should Northern Spies. Pippins are dandy. Crab apples should always be used—three or four bushels to a barrel. But, looking ahead to Februaries—no McIntosh, please.

We all had a dipper of new cider right from the vat under Mr. Mosho's press before we started home, and that's right by the right hand of God as he begins His program. We left Him there, as He wasn't about to help get my barrel down cellar on two planks. But that isn't too hard to do, and I positioned it with the bunghole up, ready to bore a hole and put in a spigot. Then I pried out the bung, and now the youngsters discovered what the straws were for. There used to be a country bumpkin song in the old B. F. Keith vaudeville days about "sucking cider through a straw." From the bunghole. Little heads clustered, and soon the level in the barrel was lowered so the straws didn't reach. Which is the reason for the extra jugs of cider. Use them to fill the barrel again—not only for childhood's straws, but because when God starts His fermentation the chum will work up through the bunghole and out, and the cider fines itself.

The Thoughtful Almighty arranged things so the children don't

linger too long at the bunghole—there is a diarrhea that responds shortly and continues just about a week. It has been called "schoolteacher's surprise," because when the cider is pressed on a Saturday and children return to school on the Monday, continuity of classes is on a ten- to fifteen-minute schedule. But as the children ease off because of schoolteacher's surprise, they also ease off because God is at work. The normal and proper mutation which begins will add a tart and tangy flavor to the sweetness of newly pressed cider. By the time the diarrhea subsides, the children no longer find cider delicious, and from then on God has things to Himself, looking ahead to February. And it is wise to let Him go it. Human hands must never add anything or do anything. When somebody tries to tell you about adding raisins, and molasses, and (it's true!) even ground beef—something to speed the process and add to the effect—pay no heed. That's nonsense and blasphemy. Let God do it. Just wait. Be patient. February always comes.

There's something else. The children were taught to lay their straws up on a cellar beam after each attack on the bunghole. Remember which is yours. The towheads of yesteryear flew the coop long ago, and may never come to Maine again in cider time. But if they do—their straws are up on the beam. To each his own.

Solid Gold

Some years ago I made reference to Kin Hubbard, and got a letter right away from a woman in Idaho who wrote, "I see you mention Hubbard kin—I wonder can you tell me anything about my great aunt Adelia Thurston Hubbard who came from Maine to Idaho in 1836?" This letter was most welcome, because Frank McKinney Hubbard, 1868–1930, was an Indianapolis newspaperman who once wrote, "February is a good month to stay home and look up your ancestors." It was indeed in a February, long ago now, that I read in the paper that former president Herbert Hoover had just received from Europe two oil portraits of ancestors and they were being shown in a museum. This news pointed up to me the disturbing fact that I don't have any portraits of my ancestors, but then I had the redeeming reflection that I don't need any. Any of our ancestors who amounted to anything are etched deep into family recollections and will live forever as surely as anything ever done in oils. When our family home burned in 1919, anything we may have had in the way of pictures and portraits was lost and cannot be replaced. An exception, I think, is a waif of a Kodak "blueprint" that shows my father in the uniform of a conductor on the Boston Elevated Railway. Dad was never all that proud of his brief experience with the "El," and didn't have much to say about it, but somehow the snapshot survived. Just before he decided to quit the El and move back to his native Maine, there was an incident few others, I think, can associate with their forebears. He was called onto the carpet in the super's office because his car ran two minutes late onto the siding at Braves' Field. He explained that it took a little extra time to collect fares on a car that seated 34 and was carrying 237 passengers, but this won him no sympathy and he felt his future lay otherwise. I do have some other snapshots of Dad, but none that enhances him as an ancestor. I have, too, a picture of my Civil War grandfather, Thomas. He is sitting on the ground in company with three regiments from Pennsylvania, two from Massachusetts, and his own 16th Maine. He couldn't tell, himself, which soldier was he. That's about it, and the only other pictures we have of ancestors are in the mind's eye.

I never set eyes on Aunt Aphia, but I have no trouble seeing her from the family tales. Black-haired, high cheekbones, lips ready to smile, and store-bought teeth that had wintered outdoors. She tossed a glass of drinking water through her bedroom window onto the lawn just before she went to bed, and her teeth were soaking in the glass. Forgetful of her. That night it snowed two feet and Aunt Aphi gummed a long winter until March lowered the snowbank. Then, I am old enough to remember one of the tintypes that perished in the fire. Anybody who ever saw it would never forget it. It was in a frame on the parlor mantelpiece, prominent. It showed a purposeful-looking old goat with a wiry mustache and mean and beady eye. The firm chin suggested a badman of the wild and roaring west, one dedicated to the extermination of Indians. Grim and dour. Could even have been a bloody pirate rampant on the Spanish Main. Fierce. But it was instead a picture of sweet and lovable Aunt Martha, a gentle and kind woman who never had chick nor child but lavished her love on nephews and nieces and was a paragon of virtue and a queen among women. Aunt Martha was solid gold. So the tintype of memory proves that

portraits reveal only faces, and the solid and honest Aunt Martha is far better remembered by hearsay and legend. At the time I saw her tintype, Grandfather assured me Aunt Martha did have a mustache. He said she also smoked a pipe.

There never was a tintype of my own great-grandmother—a Coombs from Georgetown. She had three children when she was seventeen. Since she came at that age to live in a log hut and fulfill all the obligations of a pioneer mother and ancestress, it is unreasonable to picture her in lace cuffs and puffed sleeves—as I understand prevail in the Hoover oils. It is hard to suppose she rocked gently as she hummed an honored hymn and tatted tidies for the teas she would give in the parlor. She never had a parlor. Great-Grandmother was a beefy, muscular babe, remembered as pleasing to look at in the face, but otherwise suited to her duties about the homestead. She was, we know, handy with an ax, and shoulder to shoulder with my great-grandfather she logged off 150 acres of old-growth pine in three years, to clear the farm on The Ridge. She did take a few moments from her work for her fourth and fifth children, but not enough time to slow down the clearing of fields significantly. We know that she could pick up the butt end of a downed log and roll it off the stump. She ran a good house and wandering Indians never went away hungry. She fed a good many of them in her time, and in her old age cherished, and smoked, a huge calumet that had been given to her ceremoniously by Chief Malanock of the Sabattus. One time Great-Grandmother was twitching logs, and an ox stumbled and broke his leg. She slaughtered the beast on the spot and dressed him out so the meat wouldn't spoil. So she wasn't an ancestor of frills and furbelows and flounces, out of a bandbox. She spent one whole summer laying stone wall by the south meadow.

We have no portrait of my great-grandfather, either, and can picture him only as a worthy husband of a noble wife. Maybe a part of every February should be spent wondering what the ancestors think about us.

More or Less

A picture window is an investment of merit, and in the absence of more strenuous exercise during the winter, and lacking more salubrious vistas, I look through my picture window and season my discontent with meditation and reflection. I had just finished reading in the paper that the bank had foreclosed again on the farm next below, so I've been sitting and looking the place over, and thinking that ought to teach the bank a good lesson. On the other hand, that farm has been foreclosed on every year or so now for quite some time, and I surmise bankers are hard to convince. But each new owner seems able to get a loan, and then last long enough to get foreclosed on. You can see that having a picture window is as good as magic casements opening on the foam. The farm in context used to be owned by my half great-uncle, one Jacob, who never owed anything to a bank, and during the succession of mortgages in the meantime our family has always called it the "Uncle Jacob Place."

In Uncle Jacob's time it was a beautiful piece of property. Uncle Jacob was a fussy, meticulous man who always kept everything just right. Most farm dooryards in Maine get to be lumpy, with machinery parked, hens loose, and a clothesline hanging with drawers. Not Uncle Jacob's—he was "nasty-neat" and always kept everything in its place. Never did his buggy sit out overnight—it was always backed into the shed and a robe laid over it to frustrate the dust. His hens were always in their pens. His wash line was enclosed by a latticework fence painted white, and he grew scarlet runner beans by it in the summer. If the wind took out a pane of glass, he was right there to putty it back—another farmer might wait to do that after haying was finished. Uncle Jacob's woodpile was always squared off as if plumbed; the ends of the sticks looked as if he washed them. He painted his house and barn a side a year, so in four years he had gone around and could start again. Most of the houses on our road hadn't been painted since Nero was a pup, and that Nero was long gone. Uncle Jacob's bean-poles were all the same height. He always started haying on July 5th, weather agreeable, and planned to finish on the 15th. In his flocks, every rooster had the same number of hens. As I learned from family lore, Uncle Jacob was an Old Woman, what they called a niddy-noddy. Fussy. So his fields and buildings were neat, trim, orderly—good to look across. His fences—now being meditated upon—were famous throughout the county.

Uncle Jacob cut only straight cedar down in his swamp for his fenceposts, and every post was the same height and girth. He "slarnted" off the tops, all at the same angle, so water wouldn't stand and rot the heartwood, and he trimmed knotty places with his spokeshave. He was precise with his lines and his corners, and every corner post was double braced. He always set the posts so when the wire was strung it was exactly on the line—not a smidgen one side or the other. He'd tighten his top strand first, so when he got all the wires on the fence might have been played like a zither, and if a tree came down he'd be right there the next day to work the tree up into firewood—sticks exactly sixteen inches long—and to restring the wires. Accordingly, Uncle Jacob's fences were famous throughout the region, and Robert Frost would have put him in a poem. "A good neighbor who makes good fences," he would have sung.

Uncle Jacob has been long gone for lo these many, but he lives on in the deeds. Every time the bank forecloses, it has to print a foreclosure notice in the papers, and this notice must describe the property. Thus, as the bankers and the delinquents have come and gone, and new mortgages replace the old ones, the refrain continues—". . . land formerly belonging to one Jacob Gould . . ." Nothing beside remains, really. The woodlot was long since stripped of lumber, and then pulpwood. The fields have come in to bushes and scrub pine. The trim buildings went swaybacked, and collapsed. The posy gardens are forgotten. No paint since, probably, the Civil War. And Uncle Jacob's fences have disappeared.

Nobody in Maine ever rewrites a deed. The deed that came with a place back in colonial days is good enough—just repeat it and put in the new owner's name. So these forceclosure notices in the paper tell us to start at a corner on the Old County Road, running northeasterly one hundred and forty rods along land now or formerly of one Hastings N. Littlehale, to a common corner with land now or formerly of one Roland Pierce, thence. Pierce and Littlehale were contemporaries of Uncle Jacob. In their time the "above described line" was plainly—even artistically—defined by a fence as tight as a drumhead, horse-high, bull-strong, and hog-tight, its wires humming in warm July and zinging in cold January. . . . "thence seventy-nine rods along Old County Road to point of beginning, being one hundred eighty acres be it the same be it more or less, said land being the same as deeded to Jacob Gould," etc.

I think it's good that every time some new owner sticks the bank again, Uncle Jacob gets his name in the paper. There are different ways to be remembered, and Uncle Jacob is not forgotten. Be it the same be it more or less.

Stroke for Stroke

'Twas one of our good, refreshing, State-o'-Maine northeast snowstorms that made a man of my father, and I cherish the memory of his telling about it—frequently. 'Twould never have happened had he gone south for the winter. He was eleven, going on twelve, at the time, and it was back in the days when people could work out their taxes. His father, my grandfather, didn't believe in working off the farm on principle, and often said that if anybody farmed successfully he was always too tired to work for somebody else. Henry Ford, back in Tin Lizzie days, offered a philosophy that a good American should have one foot on the land and the other in industry—that he ought to work for Henry Ford making automobiles, and then have a place big enough to keep a cow and a few hens, bringing his family up close to nature. Grandfather, who was still around in Henry's day, hooted at that. Farming, he held, didn't permit side jobs. The only exception Gramps allowed was to do something for the town and get credit on the tax bill. Most of the farmers in his day did work out some of their taxes, cutting bushes along the roads after the hay was in, maybe working on the roads with horses and dumpcart. Those who lived next to schoolhouses could go every morning to light the fires in the potbellies, and they'd get fifty cents a week credit for that chore. Cash was never that easy to come by, and every little bit helped. But Gramps insisted a true farmer would do all his business on his own place. True, he was a Civil War veteran who was exempt from taxes, and he got his pension, but that needn't tarnish the truth of his opinion. The only time Gramps relaxed his rule was when a winter storm closed off his road, and then he would turn out willingly to shovel.

There was a place between our farm and the schoolhouse, near the top of the hill, where snow drifted like sin. The land sloped just so and the woods stood close, and the situation lifted the wind so snow would dump and obliterate the road. In those times snow was important for winter hauling, and a reasonable quantity was no hardship. But horses and oxen couldn't wallow through the big drifts by the schoolhouse, and men with shovels were needed. The going rate, to be applied to taxes, was one dollar a day for an able man and fifty cents a day for a boy—a boy was anybody big enough to shovel but not big enough to be worth a dollar. Grandfather, when he went to "clear road" always took his dollar a day in cash, but true to his principle he needed that stretch of road to get his baled hay to the railroad teamtrack and his cordwood to customers "up to the city." And butter and eggs to the stores. And on this particular day he arrived to "work out," and he brought with him little Frankie, who was going on twelve. They were soon hard to work along with a couple of dozen other men and boys.

It had been a rouser of a storm and the snow was deep. So deep that a man would shovel up, another would pass along, and a third man would heave the snow over the top. By nooning, the job was better than half done, and the road commissioner knew he would have the road ready for teaming well before dark. Grandfather and little Frankie shoveled all day, side by side, stroke for stroke, and thus it was.

Along in mid-afternoon, the road commissioner, who was Harry Blethen, came along and put a hand on Grandfather's arm, causing him to pause with his shovel. "Tom," he said, "when you put in your bill to the town, set Frankie down for man's wages—he's kept up with you all day and he's worth it."

Thus my father became a man. It gave him a good feeling, and many's the time he repeated the details to me. I have no idea at just what moment I changed from a boy to a man, and I'm sure not many do, but my father could peg his moment precisely.

There is one thing to be added to this story. Dad didn't add it for a long time, and then one day we had another old ripper of a northeast blizzard, and he did. This addition may detract a mite from Dad's becoming a dollar-a-day man, but it does show that Gramps knew a thing or two. Politics, is what it was. It seems that after they'd been shoveling an hour or so that day, man and boy and side by side, Gramps turned to Mel Ordway, who was shoveling on his other side, and he said, "Mel, don't you think maybe it's time the town looked about for somebody else to take over road commissioner?"

Hauling the Boat

After the summer people were gone and we didn't miss them so very much any more, one of the last things to do before winter settled in was to haul the boat. It was something of a job then, and I admire modern times for the much improved methods of hauling a boat. Today they jerk the thing up onto a trailer with a pickup truck and yank it through town at 60 mph to horse it up on the front lawn. Alongshore, about every house has a boat by the front steps by Christmas, all ready to snake back to tidewater for spring fishing. It wasn't always so. We used to bring the boat in at high tide so it was over its cradle, the cradle being loaded with rocks so it wouldn't float. Then we'd jockey the boat into the cradle as the tide ebbed, and everybody and his odd uncles would come to jimmy and prize and lever the cradle on rollers up the beach where the highest tides couldn't reach it. It was on the day of hauling the boat that Joe came home.

It's a family story. Joe and his father, Big Joe, went to fight the French in 1759. Big Joe was a soldier, all right enough, but Little Joe, the one we're talking about, was only thirteen years old, but big for his age, and he went as a mess boy. We had an aunt in the family who wasn't quite satisfied with "mess boy" as a title of honor, so she used to explain that Little Joe really went along because his father was elderly and infirm, and the family thought he shouldn't go off to war alone. Without somebody to look after him, he might get hurt. Little Joe's father was, at the time, hale and hearty and just thirty, so he was neither elderly nor infirm. He lived to be ninety-four years old, and never had a sick day in his life. He died by an unfortunate accident—he was kicked in the head by a horse while he was twitching logs. The truth was (I had it from my grandfather) that thirteen was too young for a boy to be listed in the company records of the militia as a soldier, so all the underage volunteers were taken along as mess boys, horse grooms, and orderlies. The two Joes went first to Acadia and took part in the fracas at Louisburg. The father had a musket that was issued in the Seven Years War that was, and still is, known as a Queen's Arm, but the son, being a mess boy, was unarmed. After the jolly good fun at Louisburg, General Wolfe moved his forces up the St. Lawrence River for his attack on Quebec City, and both our Joes attended the entire performance. Little Joe was gunner for the small cannon used for the initial venture against the citadel.

Most of the "English" were farmers and fishermen from Maine, and they arrived to establish themselves at Point Levis, which is on the southern shore of the St. Lawrence across from Quebec City. From their position they could look up and see the fortress on the promontory, and they bided while General Wolfe occupied himself with his plans to attack and take the fort. Meantime, a small cannon brought along from Louisburg had been set up, and Little Joe wanted to touch it off. General Wolfe told him not to hurry things, that in time the cannon would be put to good use, but for now it wasn't heavy enough to send a ball across the river. This teased Little Joe to wonderment, and to ease the inactivity of biding at Point Levis he got another mess boy to help him, and they loaded the little cannon. Then they touched it off. General Wolfe had been right. The ball from the little cannon made a short arc out over the water and then kerplunked. There was a good splash, and when the Frenchmen up on their parapet saw the splash they cheered and waved their caps—mocking the English futility.

General Wolfe, still meditating on his plan for attack, looked up and wagged his head, remarking that "boys will be boys," and returned to his charts. After that, Little Joe and his friend had considerable amusement with the cannon, trying to find out how much powder it would take to send a ball across the St. Lawrence and into the fort. Soon they got a ball about half-way across, but it, too, kerplunked and made the Frenchmen laugh and jeer. This wasn't something that happened all at once, because by now the boys were using so much powder for each load that they couldn't fire again until the cannon had been found back in the bushes where the recoil had sent it, and until it would cool down and could be swabbed and dried for another try. Carrying the cannon to set it up again was hot work—it wasn't too heavy, but the two mess boys were only boys.

But on the third day, so Little Joe said, the boys got enough powder in the thing, and with some assurance they would reach the citadel in Quebec they applied the torch. There was a most great-grandfather of a bang that brought General Wolfe all standing from his stool. The cannon, hotter than a skunk, spun backward about ten rods. The ball carried, and it skimmed over the parapet full into the citadel of Quebec. This time nobody

looked over the parapet and jeered. And General Wolfe said, "All right, boys—you've had your fun and now let's have a little quiet about the camp."

As for the war—General Wolfe worked out a plan, arranged his soldiers, and there followed the Battle of the Plains of Abraham, at which Big Joe—Little Joe's father—was wounded. Little Joe didn't take part in the battle, because as mess boy he was expected to skirmish for food, and he and his friend were off shooting rabbits. When the boys came back from shooting rabbits they found the camp at Point Levis deserted—everybody had gone across the river and they could hear a considerable hullabaloo to show where everybody was. Later, Little Joe got across the river too, and found his dad with a musketball in his backside, and things weren't so much fun as before. He got his father back in good shape after a time, and then the two of them took the trail up the Chaudiére River and on down to the Maine coast. It was a tiring trip, particularly for Big Joe because of his bad hip, but they made it, and that has to do with hauling the boat.

It was that time of year, just before the Maine winter was due to strike, and everybody was down at the shore getting the boat up. Something like ten men were at it, with poles and rollers and blocking and pulleys and ropes, and they had two timbers laid out for working the cradle along. The tide was gone enough that they could stand under the stern, and they had so much time before the tide would be back lapping at their heels. No tractors and winches in those days. Everybody was straining, the block-and-tackle was at loggerheads, the poles weren't taking a bait, the rollers weren't rolling, nothing was going right, and nobody dared to ease off or let up and lose what purchase he had. You might say, and they would have, that they had their arse in a sling. There they were, doing every last utmost and getting nowhere and no point in yelling a bit more than they were already yelling.

And that was the day and the very moment that Big Joe and Little Joe arrived home from the battle at Quebec. Big Joe flopped on a stool at the house, and Little Joe went down to the shore to see what the noise was about. Seeing the predicament, he stepped up, added his strength to a pry-pole, and that was all the job needed. Slicker'n a schoolmarm's leg, that boat and cradle responded to that small extra push, and the boat was hauled.

Then, with the boat hauled, everybody turned and wrung Little Joe's hands and clapped him on the back and hugged him, and everybody said he was sure some old glad to see the boy home again! And this explains why, in our family, it's customary, along between Thanksgiving and Christmas, to remark that it's about time for Joe to show up. And whenever anybody is in a fix, vexed with the perversity of inanimate objects, with— as it were—his arse in a sling, it's a family tradition to look about in pathetic helplessness and ask, "Where's Joe!"

Out Having Lunch

An agreeable conversation with an amiable and intelligent neighbor smooths the rough edges of a bleak February afternoon, but you need a good wood fire in the heater and a topic that will sustain itself. Walter Garuthers, up on the Rabbit Road, drops in now and then during the winter to bring me up-to-date on his philosophies, and I have never known him to go home at dusk without leaving me a better man. When he came in this time he settled back and said, "I figured out what's wrong with them there city people."

"Oh?"

"Eyah—it's this here lunch business." For Walt, such abruptness is unusual, as he likes to work around a while before he comes to grips with a topic. So I was ready for his next remark. He said, "I been painting blinds."

"Green?" I said.

"A good green green, and I got a brush that sheds."

I said, "Brushes don't come so good lately—good brushes are hard to find."

"No, you can get good brushes if you look. But a good brush costs so much now you feel like keeping it in a vault. I sold two heifers and ten tons of hay and a barrel of pork, and then I managed to scrape up a few odd jobs that paid me well, and with a little note at the bank I managed to get a small brush to paint blinds—but it was still a cheap brush and it sheds. I had to cut down on my food some, too. Some of the blinds are

fuzzy. I had a dog once that was pup size inside and bull size outside, and he had a coat of fur rather than hair, and he never shed the way that brush does. If I had him now, I'd paint with him."

"What about these city people?"

"What city people?"

"The city people you found out what's wrong with them?"

"Oh, them—well, I been listening to the television. I set up two barrels in the kitchen, where I can be warm, and I laid down some old papers so I don't leak on the floor, and I put a blind across them barrels and I paint it. Do a side to a time. So I turn on the television, and while I don't get to see everything what with keeping my eye on the brush, I can listen, and I been listening to these playact things—thought it might amuse me. These shows where somebody is always falling on evil days and there is no profit in them, and at first I got real interested in them. I never heard one before. They're on only daytimes."

"Soap operas, they call them," I said.

"They do? Why's that?"

"Soap people advertise on them. They sell soap with the things."

"That's right—they do. They almost make me wish I had a bathtub. Well, you find out about some poor cuss who is in a peck of trouble, and while you listen a lot more happens to him, and what one day doesn't think up another day does, and he goes on and on from bad to worse. Never a happy minute in the whole show. Somebody is just out of the hospital when bang—he's in court, and then the automobile gets smashed up and the note comes due at the bank, and I found I could finish my half a blind at the rate of three disasters to one divorce."

"I never looked at one of the things."

"Sometime you should. You'll find out how lucky you are to be able to get around. So then I got to wondering whatever ails all these people, that they live that kind of way. Got to be something that goes on in the city that I wouldn't know about. And then I hit on it. I found out what ails them."

"What ails them?"

"Lunch. It's lunch. Not one of them ever gets to eat anything except lunch. Here's a man can't get along with anybody, and after everything bad happens to him he meets up with his divorced wife, who has a broken leg, and he says, 'Can't we try to make a new start? Let's have lunch and talk things over.' So they have lunch, and the restaurant catches fire. That's the way things go. Every time there's any chance to straighten things out and make somebody happy, everybody goes and has lunch. All they ever eat is lunch. Opportunity comes and bangs on the door, and there's nobody home—they're all out having lunch. Day in and day out, blind after blind, no matter how bad things get, there's always somebody having lunch. Having lunch and getting into more trouble."

"Do you have any suggestions?"

"Well, it stands to reason—what these people need is a hearty meal. If one of them ever says, 'Let's eat supper!' I'm going to take a new interest in all them problems they got. Once noontime comes and one of them playactors opens up a good old country dinner bucket, they'll find the clouds will open up and the sun'll come out. Nobody feels like making trouble on a full stomach. You want to hear something?—one day this fellow comes in and tells about something that happened at *luncheon!* *Luncheon?* What's a grown man eating luncheon for? Why don't he set himself down and tuck away a real meal like a human being? What them jokers need is some baked beans and brown bread, a few green peas and hot biscuits, now and then a beef stew with hot apple pie. They'd cure all them woes soon enough."

"The way you talk," I said, "you got me working up an appetite."

"That's the trouble with them," Walt went on. "They ain't in shape to be real people. I'd stand there painting, and I'd find myself shouting back at the television set. I'd shout, 'You come up and take supper with me, and I'll show you!' And it's the truth—I'd put them to cutting bushes and splitting wood, and hoeing down the barn, and even painting blinds, and come time to eat they'd want something better than a cussid lunch!"

I said, "I think you've hit the nail on the head."

Walt said, "Could be. I got my blinds done, anyway. I had my three squares a day, and the only thing I could think of to complain about was the way my brush molted. I never stooped to a lunch yet, and I don't aim to."

When Walt pulled on his mackinaw and started home, I stood by my kitchen window and watched him walk down the driveway into the sunset. It was a good sunset, deep red that would dissolve into the royal February purple. Walt was on ahead of a shadow that ran back fifty yards. I knew for a fact things were even so. Walt never had a problem bigger than a shedding paintbrush, and I am fortunate to have a neighbor who shares his thoughts with me.

All the Same

Now it so happens that every September a certain number of our seasonal residents will say, as they leave,
"If you happen down our way this winter, look us up!" Sometimes they add, "Of course, we'll be in Florida after the first of
the year!" It isn't often anybody takes them up on this, but
there is the story of the time Budgie Howland went down to
New York to a sportsman's show, and he decided to look up a
sport he'd been rowing around Cupsuptic Lake for the past
seventeen salmon seasons. The sport was surprised to see him,
but glad, and the guide stayed for supper and had a good time.
When Budgie got back to Rangeley he was telling about his
experiences, and he said, "And then we had a cocktail and we
had some horse's doovers."

This was allowed to sink in, and then Budgie said, "That's
French for eating between meals."

There is another story about Mr. and Mrs. Charlie Harpoon,
say, who did some bed-and-breakfasts, and one time their guests
said, "Now, if you're down our way . . ." So after cold weather
set in, Charlie said to his wife, "Just for the hell of it, why
don't we go down to Connecticut and have a weekend with
them?" So they sent a postcard and got ready to go. The only
other time Charlie and his wife had been away from home was
on a Grange hayride picnic to Sabbath Day Lake, which was
before they were married, so they looked forward to this. Charlie
got Ned Nadeau to come and do the barn chores, and Ned's

wife was going to water the house plants, and before sunup on a Saturday morning Charlie and his wife got in the pickup truck and drove off. The pickup was on the elderly side, so Charlie coasted down the hill until it coughed and started. They got to Connecticut that evening, all right, and while the aforesaid hosts now wished they'd kept their big traps shut, they welcomed the Harpoons and said they were glad to see them. Charlie and his wife were shown to a pleasant room, and after a good supper and some chit-chat they went to bed.

In due time, which was 4:30 A.M., Charlie came to and bounced out of bed to get dressed. Then he realized that his cows were at a distance and he might just as well have stayed abed. But habit dictated, so he spent the next three hours looking out windows and wishing he was home. His wife spoke to him now and then, indicating she was awake but willing to stay where she was. It was about eight o'clock when Charlie heard movement somewhere in the house and went to find his hostess up and in the kitchen. After preliminary matutinal greetings and a query about how he slept, a conversation ensued which went like this:

HOSTESS: Will you eat an egg, Charles?
CHARLIE: Eat a *what?*
H: An egg.
C: A hen's egg?
H: Yes.
C: I'll eat six of them.
H: Six?
C: Yes, I always eat six eggs.
H: Every morning?
C: Well, every morning I don't have something else. Some mornings I have pork chops and fried potatoes, and things like that.
H: I don't have any pork chops.
C: That's all right. I'll have six eggs.
H: But I got only one egg apiece!

C: You bought only four eggs?

H: Yes—I thought that would be enough.

C: How does anybody buy four eggs?

H: We can. Eggs are expensive down here, and I didn't think I'd need a dozen.

C: I could eat a dozen right now.

H: Well, you're going to get just one, and I'm sorry. You country people don't know what we city people have to pay for eggs! They don't grow on trees, you know.

C: Eyah—I know that. You city people don't know, I guess, what an egg costs me.

H: You have your own hens.

C: Right, but eggs don't grow on bushes up my way, either. How much do you think six eggs cost *me?*

H: I wouldn't have any idea. How much?

C: Well, I got five hundred hens, more or less, and right now they're on the tail end of their stretch and they go into the soup factory next week. So I have to keep feeding them, and last Friday I got five eggs from five hundred hens. Next week my pullets ought to come in, so I can start all over again. But I can show you my feed bills. Right now, eggs cost me $27.50 apiece.

H: Aw, c'mon!

C: God's truth! And when the pullets start, they lay peewee eggs, and instead of six, I take nine. Nine cost me about the same. Maybe anybody who keeps hens in Maine should come down to Connecticut to buy his eggs.

And so on. Charlie and his wife came home on Tuesday and said they'd had just the most wonderful time! Really got acquainted with the summer people. Right good sort, once you get to know them! More people, Charlie said, ought to take advantage of that come-and-see-us invitation. Find out how the other half lives. Charlie told me, "I stretched that egg stuff some— at the time my eggs was costing me maybe four dollars apiece. But for all them people know about hens, it was all the same."

Her Daily Drink

Our family cow of my youth—in a way she was *my* cow because I had to take care of her—never had advantages, and contributed liberally to both my welfare and my education without benefit of the great modern dairy knowledge that now surrounds us. In the winter, when I am comfortable in my latter-day ease, and I sit snug inside to look out upon the beautiful snowdrifts, I recall the stalwart adventures of keeping a cow—and in particular the daily afternoon chore when I had to take Blackie for a drink. She *was* black—of a breed now almost forgotten, a black Jersey. Think of Jerseys, the creamy cattle that originated on the Channel Isle, and you think of small yellow-brown animals admired by butter makers. But there was also a black throw-off, or sport, or mistake, that made just as good butter, and one of them kept me off the streets and out of the pool halls when I was in my formative years. It was my morning and evening privilege to fondle Blackie until the pail was full, and every afternoon I had to lead her from her manger to a tub in our backyard where she would drink water. In the winter, with the snow deep and the thermometer down, this was much like Peary's dash to the Pole, and I would sit in school all day and dread the moment.

The caper amounted almost to a ceremony. I had to get the snow away from the tie-up door and from the cellar-way bulkhead, and then bring the hose up from the cellar. The tub, by the bulkhead, was a good hundred yards from Blackie's tie-up. Blackie was thirsty, and while I worked the snow shovel and tangled with the hose, she would blat to keep me informed of her desires. Cows are creatures of habit, so I didn't have to lead Blackie forward or back. She knew the route. When there had been a new fall of snow, Blackie would bound out the tie-up door to discover it, and there was always a hesitation. Then she would sniff the new snow, remember that she was thirsty, and she would plunge ahead. The gigantic shudder that always shook Blackie's frame at this plunge led me to conclude that there is something about rubbing snow on your lacteal equipment. The design of a milking cow is such that she tends to drag at a vulnerable spot, which accounted for the twang that came from her tail when she plunged forward. I would follow along while Blackie waded the drifts.

While she was having her fill, I would pull the hose back into the cellar, close the bulkhead doors, and stand by until she finished. It is my recollection that a bitter northwest wind straight down from Canada always attended these exercises. Then Blackie would turn and go back to the tie-up, and I'd dump out any water that was left in the tub. I remember distinctly that sometimes the water I dumped out would have little crystals of ice in it—it had begun to freeze that soon. When Blackie got back to the tie-up she'd shiver for a time, and then she'd warm up and the stable would subside. I'd give her some cut-up potatoes or turnips, maybe a few cut-up apples, and she'd make that last until she got her dish of grain at milking time.

So you can understand why I was interested to read in a farm magazine just the other day that a dairyman down south somewhere had experienced an interesting problem with his herd. His cows fell off. This is farm talk, and means that the production of milk declined. At first the statistics were mild, and the man supposed there might have been no more cause than inferior roughage, or perhaps some sour silage—maybe

the grain had skipped an ingredient. He expected things would right themselves. But the milk continued to fall off, and in a few days things were serious.

In my time, if Blackie had any kind of a problem, we went at it in a folksy way. We'd scratch her between the horns, which cows like, and talk to her. Ask her why she's unhappy. One thing we usually did was give her a pail of warm water with a handful of ginger in it. I never knew why we did that, but we did. Then sometimes we'd look to see if she'd lost her cud. Cows ruminate, and if somehow the cud got misplaced it would upset the routine. There was a way to provide a fake cud and to present it, and then things would get better. If things didn't get better, we would call a "vet," who would come and prescribe warm water with ginger in it, or a fake cud. In my adventures, Blackie never had any disorders that didn't work themselves off, and if I didn't give her too many cut-up turnips all at once she'd go a long time without disorders. But nowadays dairy farming is in the big business bracket, and any kind of a disorder verges on the catastrophe. This farmer down south was beside himself. His herd enjoyed every privilege. Where poor old Blackie had a tie-up, his cows lounged in sumptuous boudoirs. They had a milking parlor with clinically precise equipment—the milk piped to a sterile receiving room and handled all the way by computer circuits. Diet, and every care, was right on button every minute. Each cow had her separate apartment, with separate manger to which food came automatically, and her own private drinking fountain—when she pressed her muzzle into the fountain it gurgled until she was replete and then it shut itself off. Unless you've seen modern cow in her high estate, you won't believe how far we've come since the days of poor Blackie. No cow, today, ever drags her keel in a snowbank.

Well, this farmer down south couldn't figure out his problem. He called in his vet (nowadays vets are on full-time contract and have assistants) and extensive tests were made. The vet was puzzled and called in the state department of animal husbandry. A specialist came from the experimental farm, and another from the extension service. A call was put in to Washington. But every time a milking machine was taken off a cow, she showed she was down again from yesterday. The farmer faced bankruptcy. His monthly check from the creamery dropped to $32.25. The vet suggested "salvage value" at the slaughterhouse.

Then, this magazine told me, everything was explained. The farmer, as a last resort, checked out the drinking fountains. He shoved his hand into one, to see if the valve was working, and he was much astonished when a jolt of red-hot lightning went up inside his sleeve and knocked him sprawling to the other side of the barn. He felt a lot like a high tension line, and he lit up like a toaster. But in his eyes was another light—the light of understanding. Some dolt, probably himself, had grounded the milking machine circuit to the water pump. Since that, no cow had taken on any water.

True, Blackie lacked many comforts, and her daily drink at the wintry tub was an ordeal—for her and for me. But she got her water every day, and as boss of the works I knew she did. The way she shivered back in the tie-up—so did she.

Far More Smug

All manner of things need our attention and some of them deserve it, so I like to sit around on these pleasant winter afternoons and think about them. I get up every so often and put another stick in the stove, and look out the window at the blue jays, and than I sit down and think some more. I've been thinking about this item in the newspaper that says it gets easier and easier to become a member of the Mayflower Society. I hadn't been thinking all that much about it up to now, but it does seem reasonable. My first reaction is to consider this a great pity, because we need something in this country that everybody can't have. Democracy is all right, and should be supported, and there is a valuable challenge in the fact that every native-born boy and girl has the same right to grow up and be president of the United States. It refreshes our faith in our way of life to reflect that some of them, however improbable, have even done it. But there is likewise a worthy challenge in the Mayflower Society, to which even the wealthiest, mightiest, most erudite, finest favored boy and girl—even the president of the United States—cannot aspire unless he (she) is descended from a true Plymouth Pilgrim, and can prove it. Perhaps I see things aslant, but I'm glad we have a Mayflower Society.

And it's this matter of proving your ancestry that is now being considered. Myself, I'm not worried. Some of my aunts belonged to the Mayflower Society, and also the Daughters of the American Revolution, so I happen to know I am eligible to the first, if not the second. Perhaps I ought to be awaiting eagerly the glorious day when our Supreme Court, in its finite wisdom, orders the Daughters of the American Revolution to dis-sex themselves and take in gentlemen daughters. Perhaps, too, by that time we will be totally American and the Daughters will, like our Congress and our colleges and our bus stations, extend trisexual membership and have done with distinctions. Anyway, I could, if I wanted to, take on the Mayflower Society— one of my grandfatherly ancestors tangled with a granddaughter of Elder Brewster who made him a good wife and his children a good mother. The fact that I have never applied for membership is my own business, and I'm not about to discuss business at this time.

What makes it easier to join the Mayflower Society now is the proliferation of generations. As everybody is presumed to be descended from Noah and spouse, so in time everybody will be descended from a Mayflower member. There were twenty-two families on the Mayflower, and by applying the simple Malthusian theory of geometrical progression there has got to come a time when enough nonmember Mayflower descendants marry Mayflower descendants to equal the thing off at fifty-fifty. Next, the one 50 percent would marry the other 50 percent and we'd have a population that runs 100 percent Mayflower. When that happens, more or less on a natural biological schedule, the special exclusive nature of the Mayflower Society will cease to have an appeal. Anybody can join. And the original twenty-two Mayflower families can blame nobody but mathematics, sex, and themselves. The very aristocracy that started the society will have bred itself into democratic conformity. There's going to be a day when it will be far more smug to brag about coming from a long line of smugglers, pirates, and convicted felons.

There's another thing about this—the way records are kept.

In the old days when somebody wanted to prove he was descended from a Mayflower family, he had to hunt through musty old vital statistics—sometimes hiring a professional archivist to explore for him. There was this begat and that begat, and slowly the kinships were fathomed and there you were— you could join the Mayflower Society. But now all the true lines from the wellspring have been traced, and it gets harder and harder to find somebody who is not a Mayflower descendant.

Still thinking—won't it be fun when the Supreme Court does tell the D.A.R. to open up?

A Vigorous Sport

One of our esteemed summer visitors came in to borrow a screwdriver, and his remarks included that every winter down in Florida he plays a lot of shuffleboard. I thought he said *shuttleboard*, but he didn't. I upped him by saying my winters have been running to Ping-Pong, and I found it a vigorous sport. He didn't seem inclined to argue about this, so I let it go. I'm not all that much on Ping-Pong, but I did make a Ping-Pong table some years back, and now and again we dust it off for want of other excitement.

I had heard of Ping-Pong. Mostly, from young folks who went away to college and took up frivolities. Les Grondin told me if he'd-a knowed his boy was swatting a whing-dingus back and forth with a sandpaper bat, he'd-a kep' him to home and taught him to sort sawdust. Les said first time he ever heard of Ping-Pong, he thought it was a foreign language, like maybe Hong Kong, or perhaps like Greek or Calculus. I sympathized with

Les, because the first time I saw a Ping-Pong ball I wondered how long a guinea hen would sit on a dozen of them before giving up. Then, knowing something about guinea hens, I laughed to myself, because a good guinea hen would probably hatch the things. I've always had a secret desire to toss a guinea hen's egg onto a Ping-Pong table during a fast match and see what happens.

I never supposed that Ping-Pong would insinuate itself into our normal, well-oriented, conservative, down-Maine household, and wasn't ready when it did. The lad said, affecting an aggrieved and abused air, that other people had Ping-Pong tables and he felt our household would become more meaningful if we did. I said I'd heard quite a few foolish remarks that day, first to last, but that was certainly the peachiest, and why didn't he go and help his sister with the dishes? But he made a big case for Ping-Pong, and as I had grown into the habit of blaming everything on the schools I asked his teacher what about this Ping-Pong? She said Ping-Pong was a fine game.

It teaches coordination, I learned, and improves dexterity, enhances footwork, contributes to vigor and appetite, relaxes tired muscles, lifts the attitudes, and promotes good sportsmanship. So does fetching up a calf, but I could see I was licked. I looked in the mail order catalog to see what a Ping-Pong table looks like, and when I saw the price I decided to make one. Word went around town that I was making a Ping-Pong table, and a few people came to see if that were so. They told that I was, sure enough, and one man said, "Ain't likely he'd say he was if he warn't." I surmise it was the words ping and pong— it isn't easy to dignify them. Ping. Pong. When I went to the hardware store the good old gang was there, and until now the boys had always greeted me with enthusiasm and respect. Now things were different. One of them said, "Care to ping for us a little bit?" Then the others said "Ha!" several times over and a hilarity prevailed. I asked the storekeeper what kind of paint I ought to get for my Ping-Pong table.

"Green," he said.

Then somebody said, "Ought to be a flat paint—ha, ha, ha, ha, ha!"

"Have your fun," I said. "But do I use a stain, an enamel, common blind paint, or what?"

In due time we assembled to give Ping-Pong a fair try. I found Ping-Pong runs mostly to swatting a whing-dingus back and to with a sandpaper bat, and that younger people are not only more agile at it than I am, but take to it with greater zeal. It may be my advancing years will keep me from winning too many championships. I hope so. But the rascals do give me a workout now and again, and there's really no need for me to go to Florida to play shuffleboard.

Prout's Portias

I t does seem that in the small Maine towns that have been cajoled into zoning ordinances, and other improvements, most of the agitation started with folks from away who settled in to get here from wherever they were, and now want to wreak reforms and make the lovely old village a decent place to live. So one of our winter duties is to peruse the annual town report, not just to find out what went on, but to surmise about next year's oddities. Town meeting comes in March, and while the social life of a community moves on its own pleasant schedule, the official affairs stem from and flow toward annual town meeting. It is not to be taken lightly, and with all the new ideas about community betterment, town meeting needs all the help it can get. Truth is that with every new and wonderful ordinance we strangle some more of the one-time strength that made our town meeting the last fortress of real political freedom in an otherwise muddled world. Oh, we might have been better off with a few well-thought-up restrictions back along, and then again . . .

What came to mind as I was looking at this year's town report with its usual proposals for community betterment was the effort made so many years ago to zone John Prout's slaughterhouse, and how reason prevailed and justice triumphed when the do-gooders tried to run him out of business. John was the town butcher and had taken over the business from his father, who had taken it over from *his* father, so you can see that the Prout slaughterhouse was well established in the community. Lest sensitive folks presume otherwise to the detriment of John's reputation, let it be known that he was all the same a mild-mannered man, soft-spoken and moderate in his thoughts and actions. He had a college diploma, in Latin, on the wall behind his desk in the butchery. He supported the church and sang a good tenor in the choir. Were you to see him walking past without knowing his trade, you might take him for a retired teacher of instrumental music in a select seminary for females, and nobody would ever take him for the finest meatman in miles around. The Prout homestead stood on a knoll just above the town's "corner," which is important because the slaughter-house was to the rear and thus close to the center of town. John lived—at that time—in the house with his wife Mary and three daughters aged fifteen, seventeen, and nineteen. The daughters were three of the most beautiful young ladies any-body ever clapped an eye to—two of them lived at home and attended the local school and the oldest was a normal school student in the next town.

It should be remembered that in those times a slaughter-house was important to a town. Life centered within the com-munity more than it does now, and a main street needed a blacksmith, a grocer, a doctor, a milliner, a hardware store, and certain other services along with a good abatoir, and John Prout was respected. And, besides being a good butcher, he was fair with his prices. He belonged to the days when almost every home produced some of its own meat, so John was essential to the hogs and chickens and veal and whatever else was to be "hung" for family use.

So there came to town a fastidious element that marched to new drummers, and one year there appeared in the warrant for town meeting an article that would create zoning ordinances. As often happens, too many people presumed this wasn't going to change things too much, so there was a desultory interest, and the moderator was obliged to declare that the article had been passed. The next thing of importance that happened was that John Prout was asked to move his objectionable slaughterhouse from its three-generation location to some distant, and unspecified, place where it would no longer disturb the serenity of the community. At this the slumbering interest in zoning awakened, and people realized that zoning doesn't have to be all good. John Prout paid no immediate heed, but soon papers were served on him to cease and desist, and his business was said to be unsanitary, unhealthy, and a public nuisance. At this, John Prout told his critics to go and do thus and so, which was strong language for a good man, but he was agitated with cause and we should forgive him.

Then some more papers were served, and John Prout was ordered to appear in court to show cause, etc., and ordered to comply or suffer the full penalty of the zoning ordinances as made and provided. So John Prout was to confront a jury of his peers at the county seat, and there didn't seem to be much on his side. The zoning ordinances, a lot of people agreed, like most zoning ordinances in Maine, had their absurdities, but they were part of the deal and had been enacted in proper form. It was just too bad for slaughterhouses that stood that close to the decent part of town. The do-gooders were confident, and the town was certainly on its way to a new and glorious era of reform. Now, a few days before the big case was to come up in court, John Prout took the steamcars and went to Boston to do a little shopping. He came home with boxes and boxes of whatever he bought, and it was load enough so Henny Prescott from the livery stable took an express wagon to bring the boxes to the Prout house.

And after John Prout had been arraigned in court for his heinous crime of defiling the village, the county attorney bore down hard and proved beyond any question that John Prout was guilty as charged. As there hadn't been much in the way of crime in the county for some years, the county attorney was glad for a chance to show off, and he lingered and took advantage of his opportunity. And just as he was at the peak of his brilliant presentation, the courtroom door opened and in came the three Prout daughters, fifteen, seventeen, and nineteen—Alice, Deborah, and Agatha. They moved in stately grace down the center aisle of the courtroom, approaching His Honor on the bench, and then they turned and sat down beside their father. John Prout rose and bowed, showing extreme pride in their appearance. They certainly did look some good.

Because what John Prout had bought on that shopping trip to Boston had been boxes and boxes of new clothes for his three lovelies, and here they were—gowned like queens in the latest style, three of the most beautiful maidens ever to grace a judicial scene in the history of the State of Maine. It was a fact that His Honor looked down with his jaw gaped open, and the county attorney stood entranced with one finger in the air and an interrupted furthermore on his silent tongue.

It was now that John Prout said in his quiet, female-seminary kind of voice—although he was heard all over the courtroom— he said, "I ask you, Your Honor, if *they* look unhealthy and unsanitary?"

And that was that. The zoning ordinances stayed on the books because they had been lawfully enacted, but nobody paid any attention to them. If anybody mentioned zoning, after that, he would get, "Unhealthy! Haw, haw!" So John Prout continued to butcher on the knoll above the village and he finished out his days. He would say now and then that the hats and gowns for the girls cost him a good deal less than a lawyer.

A Natural Mistake

Concerning summer people, I should mention the skunk. People who go south for the winter don't know about our skunks of the January thaw—January being the time we see more skunks than not. Skunks do not go south for the winter, but hibernate close to home in a hole in the ground. Because skunks are nocturnal and forage afield, we don't run into many of them in the summer—it's in January that they wander close to buildings and become prominent. All Maine skunks remove themselves when the weather chills and go to sleep in a den to live on residual fat and await the joyous springtide. They seem to forget about our January thaw.

The January thaw of this particular year came on the wings of a southerly breeze and brought the thermometer up about twenty-five quick degrees. It rained all night. This took off most of the snow, leaving some around the edges of the fields and behind the buildings. This caused our little friend to rouse, and when he got a whiff of good warm air he imprudently surmised that spring had come and it was time for him to be up and about. Still half asleep, our little skunk came up from his hole and was delighted that the snowbank had gone and that fragrant balms of delight were being wafted in from Bermuda. He hurried forth with eager appetite to see what he might devour. It was a natural mistake. He would soon learn the difference and go back to resume his hibernation, but for an hour or so he is beguiled. A lot happens in that hour or so.

The skunk is not, really, a bad fellow. He is maligned by some people who don't understand him, and seldom gets the approval he deserves. Popularity ought to depend on your character, reputation, usefulness, good deeds, and general appearance, and not on how you smell. A skunk eats many insects that would otherwise be nuisances. He is a better mouser than a cat, but unlike a cat seldom gets asked into the house. And the skunk is friendly. A fox keeps his distance, the squirrel sits afar, and the crow jeers from yonder oak. But a skunk will come right up under the pantry window. Anyway, this skunk I'm telling about was in our dooryard during a January thaw, not yet aware that he had been misled by a false spring, and he was looking for bugs. Our dog, who was a new dog and not informed about skunks, was asleep on the back steps. He had been attending to his duties as farm manager and custodian of the family jewels, and his repose was a deep reward for his care and concern. When the dog became aware of the skunk, he leaped into action, barked a sizable bark, and hurried to ascertain the cause of this intrusion.

The skunk won.

It's true the skunk took an unfair advantage. Instead of sneaking in as a fox would, or winging in silently like an owl, the skunk simply came. Any dedicated dog, responsibility heavy on his shoulders, is going to step right up and take charge. "Skunk about tonight," I said laconically in the bedroom, and I closed the window. Our dog felt terrible about his horrible mistake. He was filled with remorse and chagrin, which continued into August, by which month he was defused enough to be allowed back in the house. By that time he had, however, decided against skunks and he never had any further problems with them.

The little skunk, in the meantime, was much upset that he had caused our dog such anguish, and he retired shortly to his burrow to go back to sleep and wait for the true change of seasons. Within the week his hole was again under two feet of snow. So dog and skunk were better informed as a consequence, and the dooryard meeting was well worth while. But, you've got to be here in January to get the good of things like that.

No Great Favorite

The earliest known seasonal visitor to Maine was the ale-wife, and he has never been esteemed all that much either. The alewife returns about the middle of May to crowd up into our coastal streams on spawning runs, and is accordingly a harbinger. In Indian times he was esteemed mostly as encouragement under a hill of corn—the fish the Indians taught the Pilgrims to use as fertilizer. This, I've always thought, has been misinterpreted by serious historians, who seem to think this was a kind thing for the Indians to do. Instead, it was a bit of a joke on the Pilgrims by the fun-loving Wampanoags, and contributed to great hilarity in the tepees. The Indians didn't tell the Pilgrims what would happen. So when the Pilgrims did put an alewife under each hill of corn, every bobcat, skunk, fisher, mink, weasel, and raccoon in Massachusetts converged to dig up the fish. You can read about it in the Pilgrim journal, where it says, ". . . then they planted their gardens a second time and guarded them at night."

The word alewife has an interesting entry in the dictionary. It says an alewife is a woman who keeps an alehouse. Then it says an alewife is ". . . an American fish (*Pomobolus pseudoharengus)* of the herring family. It is a poor food fish." For a derivation of the second meaning, all the dictionary says is, "(perh. a diff. word)." Probably. A good guess is that the Penobscot Indians couldn't manage to handle *Pomobolus pseudoharengus,* and for some

reason called the fish an L-Y. The plural is L-Y's. News that the alewives are back brightens the May day when the villagers hear it. When alewives appear in the river it is fairly safe to lay away the snowshoes. The Maine L-Y is the Nova Scotia *gaspereau*.

In spite of being a poor food fish, the alewife gets eaten by some few who like to have him smoked. Alongshore an L-Y that is smoke-cured is called a *smoker*, and for a few weeks every spring little signs appear on fish houses, Smokers for Sale. He's bony. His flavor is not all that bad if he's served in a cream sauce on boiled potatoes, and in former times he was seen in grocery stores lined up on a stick by the dozen, and he would be offered either as a *bloater* or a *Kennebec turkey*. Down in Nova Scotia, they make cheese sandwiches—two slices of cheese with a gaspereau between. This curious custom never caught on in Maine except at Lubec. Otherwise the alewife is no great favorite with the Maine palate, and remains a good harbinger without reference to diet.

Then, tons and tons of L-Y's are netted every spring in a commercial manner and sold to lobstermen for bait. The lobstermen tell me the brim that has been put in the traps all winter has lost its appeal by May, and the lobsters are ready for a treat. I think I notice that the lobstermen, too, are ready for a change, and their winter-weary spirits are lifted when the first L-Y's appear.

The first L-Y means it won't be long now.

Had His Choice

O n the nether end of summer comes the pie season— and I assume the pie was an early Maine invention, brought to its peak of perfection as a special and merited reward for those who spend the winter. True, there are summer pies and people to eat them, but they remain in a fleeting and desultory category and perform mostly as fillers for the meantime. Pie as we perform it was never a warm weather exercise. Just before Thanksgiving our official pie season opens and pies of all sexes may be taken freely in all counties, no bag limit. The honest housewife girds her ap'n, turns up the heat, and lets herself go. Now she outdoes all her artistry of August, including May, June, July, and part of September. She did, indeed, make good ones from the juicy pie-plant, the luscious Latham, the perky August Sweet, the bouncing blueberry, and even the unlikely green tomato, but now, with a chill in the air, she settles in for the long winter of family content. Pie is our leading winter sport.

The other evening at supper, feeling sorry for the departed rusticators, and being both enthusiastic about and full of my subject, I waxed eloquent and delivered a paean for the pie, prefacing my prepared preachment with a piece of apple and a piece of mince in double harness on my plate, and referring liberally to my notes from time to time I made harangue somewhat as follows:

> Ladies and gentlemen, assembled friends, True Believers, all—behold the Pie! Or what's left of it. Observe its succulence, its art form, its nourishing capabilities, its delicate demean, its erudite composure! Do we not have a lesson here for a grieving world? Doth the pie not teach us all a great lesson? What doth better sustain us in despondency, nurture us in need, support our institutions?

I went on for quite a time, until everybody was impressed by my sincerity, and filled with emotion as well as pie. After gaining attention thus, I went on to speak of John Milton, who was a poet of some merit but an unfortunate citizen of a dark era before Maine invented pies. I mentioned a small thing he wrote which he called *Areopagitica*, a treatise that defended freedom of choice. I suggested that if Mr. Milton had known anything about pies he would have altered his text and done a much better job. How lean, indeed, was the literature of those backward times, when page after page and volume after volume of otherwise commendable reading lacked pies as we know them! What is a fatted calf without pie? Would Alfred the Great allow a *pie* to burn? Little Miss Muffet ate curds and whey? I lamented the sad aspect of Chaucer's nun, who was so fastidious while eating that never a morsel fell upon her bosom. How much more affectionately would we cherish her today (I asked) if Chaucer had permitted her to ride to Canterbury with a splash of hearty boiled cider pie on her wimple! Long before his time, Little Jack Horner pulled out a plum—and what a good boy was he!

So Poet Milton, I went on, spoke of Saint Peter, who was ordered, "Arise, Peter, slay and eat!" There was no divine instruction as to what Saint Peter was supposed to kill and what he was supposed to eat—that was left to him and that was freedom of choice. Now, does anybody doubt that Peter would have chosen pie if he had known anything about pies? But he didn't know about pies, so the story sort of peters out and we have no notion of what he slew or et. So I asked my companions to join me in a contemplation of what Poet Milton would do at a Grange supper to demonstrate his great freedom of choice:

WAITRESS, leaning over Mr. Milton from behind: What'll you have for pie?

MR. MILTON: What d'you got?

WAITRESS (proudly): Mince, apple, custard, cranberry, lemon, raisin, squash, rawzbree, peach, chocolate, butterscotch, punkin . . .

MR. MILTON: Gracious! Well, let me see—er, uh, well—why don't I have a piece of apple?

So Mr. Milton got a piece of apple, and Freedom of Choice won a notable victory.

Then I said, "Now, I'm going to ask Mother to assist me in dramatizing the facts of pie-time in the State of Maine, and you can see why Poet Milton spent a lot of time considering how his life was spent." So Mother came up behind me and made like a waitress at a Grange supper.

MOTHER: What'll you have for pie?

ME: What d'you got?

MOTHER (proudly): Mince, apple, custard, cranberry, lemon, raisin, squash, rawzbree, peach, chocolate, butterscotch, punkin . . .

ME: Yes.

So everybody could see that Poet Milton was in a sad case with his freedom of choice and was now sitting poetically with his one piece of apple pie gone and nothing to do but twiddle his thumbs until all the other people got through eating. Everybody could see that he really wanted some more pie, but he'd had his choice and there he was.

I was glad, thus, to speak a good word for pie, and I felt everybody had seen my point. Mother went back to her chair and said, "Well, he got the last piece of apple, so mince is all that's left. Who wants mince?"

But Not Quite

O ne thing we can do to while away the winter is take the census. I took it one year, but not quite. I got the idea that Uncle Sam has a hard time finding somebody to take the census, so you might say the job is open if you want it. Every ten years they take the regular census, by which Congress is apportioned, and then in five years they take the farm census, but nobody seems to know why. I took the farm census (but not quite) in 1945, and it was five years after that when the regular census began asking personal questions and everybody got mad. FDR had set up the big cradle-to-grave boondoggles, and all at once the government had to know if the people liked sugar in their tea, wore pantyhose, left the bottom button of the vest undone, and things like that, and we had about six months of splendid letters to the editor, but the questions got asked anyway. The farm census had been asking fairly personal questions, so farmers weren't so upset as some others. In 1945 when I tried to take the farm census, the country was in a bind.

Well, all the Democrats had jobs. They were running the WPA and the OPA and the CCC and for a while the NRA, and when the call went out for idle Democrats to take the census, there was a mild response. I was sitting by the stove one afternoon, rejoicing in my leisure and promising myself I would do more of it, and a white-wall Caddie came into the yard and a rich man got out of it. Through the window I could see that he was wealthy. I took him for either the president of Chase National Bank or the ambassador from India. He tapped at my front door with the business end of his ivory-headed walking stick, and when I opened he said, "Good day!"

Nobody says good day. That's like alas and zounds. Like gadzooks. But I agreed with him and he introduced himself as a coordinator for the farm census and might he come in? So we sat, and he said he had been unable to find anybody in the vicinity who would take the census, and in an extremity he had called to ask if I might have a suggestion. I told him I was a Republican, and he said he knew that. I told him I didn't know of anybody who was both a Democrat and unemployed, but I said if I thought of somebody, where could I reach him? But in a week or so I hadn't thought of anybody, so he came back. I had expected him to come back, so now I told him I might consider the job but there were two or three things I wanted understood. I told him I was doing this as a favor, and I didn't want my name in the paper so people might think I had changed my party. He nodded at this, and then I said there was a much more important matter.

"Which is?" he asked.

"Gasoline."

Those were ration days, and rural people had put up with years of damphool government regulations about gasoline. At one time I had six thousand white ration stamps, each stamp good for one gallon of tractor gasoline, and I had to write my name on each stamp when I used it. But the stamps were no good to me because there was no gasoline available. If any gasoline station in town was lucky enough to get a load of gasoline, the village people would line up with ten-gallon stamps, which they didn't have to sign, and they took all the gasoline before any farmers could get to town. Oh, yes! So ration stamps didn't mean gasoline by a long shot, and I was ready for him when this man told me he would provide all the gasoline stamps I would need to take the farm census.

I said, "I don't mean that."

I told him I still had three thousand, two hundred and eighty-nine ration stamps unsigned, and hadn't seen any gasoline in three months. Maybe it's hard today to believe those things went on. But this man promised faithfully he would personally see that I got what gasoline I needed, and then he gave me a bundle of printed instructions, another bundle of census blanks, and his chauffeur drove him away.

First, I had to go to school. The school was conducted by a Democrat who couldn't pronounce big words. All we about-to-be census takers met at the county courthouse on the appointed day, and this instructor began to read the instructions on how to take the census. When he came to a big word he would skip it. So the instructions came by spells, and he would read, "When . . . three years or under . . . second column . . . also enter in column eight . . . unless . . . if over ten in number . . . except milch goats." Then he would ask us if we all understood, and we would all say that we did.

So I got full instructions on how to take the farm census, but I didn't get any gasoline. I did get a check for four dollars for attending the school of instruction, and I frittered it away on some lavish impulse. Then I waited around for gasoline. I would get a letter from headquarters asking how I was coming along on the census, and I would mail it back with a note written across it: "Where's the gasoline?" Then I would get a letter asking if I were having problems, and when did I estimate I would complete the census?

I never did take the census. As far as I know, nobody ever

took the 1945 farm census in my town. The shortage of gasoline continued, and I managed to get through the winter without
any. I still had three thousand, two hundred and eighty-nine
white ration stamps, unsigned, and if you want to climb up on
the ladder and look on the top shelf, you'll find I still have
them. But taking the census that winter gave me something to
occupy my mind, and there is usually something like that to
turn up and help. You don't want to think we just sit around
idle.

He Meant Turnips

C levie Bickford's occasional dooryard visits were every one
a joy, and maybe I treasure most the memory of his
turnip visit the afternoon of July third. As he hopped out of
his pickup I said, "Time to plant the turnips!" In Maine we
mean rutabagas when we say turnips, and "on or about" the
Fourth of July is the time to plant. That brings them along so
they're the right size by frost, and a couple of sharp frosts before
they're pulled makes them sweet. Clevie laughed when I mentioned turnips, and he said, "We had a turnip winter when I
was a boy, and I don't care if I never see another turnip. Worst
winter of my life."

So he spun his memory of that turnip winter on the old Bickford farm up by the Fisher School, concerning himself and his
brother Theodore, and their stern father.

"Father had a pasture coming in to hardhack and junipers,
and he thought it ought to be turned over and sod-down, so
he set us boys to making a turnip piece. It plowed worse than
dragging a fishhook down a blanket, but we got it turned over

by dint of steer-sweat, and we dressed it about a foot deep, and then we wheel-harred it, and by that time we had all we wanted of turnips and still no turnips planted.

"So one morning Father said, 'Well, I guess today's as good a day to plant turnips as it is to do anything else, so why'n't you two get at it soon's you've et?' Well, we didn't think much of that, because that happened to be the Fourth of July and we had a mind to go over to Carter's Corner and see the handtubs and help with the town picnic. But when Father said turnips he meant turnips, so we hitched up and started for the piece with a bag of seed, and while we drove along we talked about the great need in our town for a machine that would plant turnips, which is a chore and a half.

"T'eo said we ought to go and rent a handtub so we could squirt the seeds. But I had me an idea, and when we came to that place in The Kingdom where the sand knoll makes out to the road, we shoveled the bottom of our cart full of sand. Then we spread a layer of turnip seed on the sand, put in more sand, spread more seed, and like o' that until we had the cart full of sand. Then we drove on to the turnip piece.

"T'eo drove the horses and I shoveled sand out over the tailgate, and we kept on until we had sand all over the piece. Then we went and saw the handtubs and helped with the picnic and had a good time, and we got home in time for chores. Father asked us if we'd seeded the turnips, and we said we had. I guess we had—that sand was a good idea. Every seed came up, I don't think a-one-on-'em skipped. We'd seeded something like four acres in maybe an hour, and in two weeks the place looked like a patch of buckwheat. Father went to look at it and said it seemed to be all right. And by September, we had a jungle of turnips that would frighten you.

"Then, after we'd had a couple of good frosts, Father said, 'Frost must-a worked some flavor into them turnips by now— don't you think you boys ought to start gatherin'?' So we started. We hauled and we hauled, and we cut tops off, and we piled the things down cellar. There was one night T'eo dreampt he was hauling turnips until he jumped out of a sound sleep yelling at the horses, and he was all tired out at breakfast. I guess I dreamed some, too, and we kept on hauling and hauling.

"Then one afternoon we were bringing our big two-hoss load home, and we met Reed Edgecomb on the road. He had a farm over the other side of us on the back road that ran to swales and sand, and he warn't known nationwide for the crops he grew. So Reed looked at our pretty load of turnips and he says, 'Where're you boys getting all them nice turnips?'

"Before T'eo could say anything, I sized things up, and I figured maybe we could get out of pulling and hauling and cutting a few turnips. So I says, 'Why, do you want some turnips?' Reed allowed he might use a few. So I said, 'Go help yourself—take all you want! Put on a good load!'

"Well, when we came back, there was Reed Edgecomb's cart stuck in the wet place on the edge of our field, and he had so many turnips on his hosses couldn't pull out. T'eo and I were only too glad to unhitch one of our team and give him some help. Wonder that load he had didn't crack his wheels. I never knew how many loads Reed took, but what he took we didn't have to pull, and between us we got that turnip piece cleaned up and then it came on to winter.

"Then one night Father said, 'I believe it's time to sell some turnips.' So the next day he took the long pung full of turnips, a blanket over them and a lantern lit under the blanket, and set out for The Falls to sell some turnips. He went to the Farmer's Union, to Heistermann's, to Marchak and Bichrest, to Plummer's, and to all the stores, and he asked if they'd like some good turnips. They all said no, that they were getting some mighty good turnips this winter, sweet and tender, all good size and firm, and they thought they'd stay with what they were getting while they lasted. So Father asked them who was selling them these good turnips, and they all said, 'Reed Edgecomb.'

"Father came home and said he couldn't sell a turnip, and he said to us, 'Where did Reed Edgecomb grow any turnips this year? I didn't know he grew any turnips.' We said we didn't know he grew any. Father said, 'Seems-so if he'd growed some turnips we'd-a knowed about it. I didn't know he growed any.' Father mentioned the matter off and on a good deal all winter, and we boys kept telling him we didn't know that Reed Edgecomb grew any turnips. We fed turnips out—pigs, cows, hens, sheep, even the hosses. And worst of all, ourselves—three meals a day, day in and day out. Then we still had a lot left over come spring. But Father never sold a one on account of Reed Edgecomb. Turnip winter, it was—worst winter I recall."

The Very Best

Now and then some gentleman who is otherwise considered erudite will say to me, "Ah! Yours is the life! I have to go back to my teeming city after joyous holiday hours, and you stay right here living like a king! Would that I could stay, too! You know how to live! Lucky you!"

And more of the same. So I will relate an amusing tale out of October—October being a truly lovely month out here in the salubrious countryside, with every last one of our seasonal visitors long gone. October, in some ways, is our best month. High blue skies, bright fallish air, color on the maples, and just about everything magnificent. I had been doing something outdoors all day, except for my meals, and was in a mood to relax in the cozy chair until beddy-bye—which would be soon. There is a way I have of sitting on the back of my neck and stretching everything down into my slippers, so the kinks and curlicues of an active day fit back into place. These kinks aren't the consequence of golf and tennis and sailing a boat, and this isn't a question of "unwinding." Unwinding is a city word. I had a book, but lost interest in turning the pages, and I had an apple ready if my strength returned to pick it up. My love had fetched me a bowl of popcorn, with plenty of butter the way I like it, and in sympathetic concern had pressed a cooling hand gently to my brow in passing, remarking that she cared enough to bring the very best. Then she returned to the kitchen to finish her wifely pursuits, and shortly I heard her say, "Dear, I can't seem to get any water!"

Oh boy! Mine is the life.

Our idyllic little home, surrounded by sylvan beauty, is not attached to a town water pipe. We have a well, and we have a reciprocating water pump, and we have me. She had been putting through a small laundry, and when she pushed the button the response was nugatory. "All I get," she called to me, "is a gurgle." I unlimbered myself from my pleasantries, murmuring a jocular "Täätschmr!" which nobody heard except me, and I went down cellar, which in our house is the opposite of going upstairs to bed. In the cellar I found my reciprocating water pump running smoothly enough, but an ear to the intake told me there was no water involved. This would explain an upstairs gurgle, but didn't tell me much else. From previous bouts with my pump, I knew the fault might be one or more of many—one time it's one thing and another time it's another, but not always. It is my practice to keep on hand what the mail order house calls a "repair kit," which is a package of washers, springs, plungers, packing, gaskets, and other untitled items. After I have used a repair kit I immediately order another, to have whatever I may need on hand for the next gurgle. I now reached my repair kit down from its shelf and went to my shop in the shed to put tools in a carry-box. This is the life! Now I began to take the pump apart, and shortly had everything spread out in orderly arrangement on the pumproom floor. Now I could put things back together and replace or fix whatever was wrong—whatever it was. I checked. I had closed the cocks, disconnected the motor, released the pressure—all seemed ready.

And now I found that instead of a repair kit for my Little Wonder Reciprocating Water Pump, the mail order house had sent me the repair kit for a Baby Giant Deep Well Injection Pump. I did not know this until just now. I had no way of knowing, down there in the pumproom, if Mr. Sears or Mr. Roebuck had done this evil deed to me, but I mentioned them both at the time, and I wondered if maybe I shouldn't have gone to spend the winter in the city.

A reciprocating pump is not too complicated, and with the right repair kit it isn't difficult to keep one running and pumping. I had no way to get another repair kit at that time of night; I had nobody to call. Mine is the life! I started warily, checking everything, and slowly put my pump together again with the same parts I took out. I oiled some things, wiped others dry, and fiddled the springs. I heard a voice from the kitchen upstairs lilting on its way to bed, "Goodnight, Irene, I'll see you in my dreams." Country boys have all the fun! I was alone with my ingenuity.

My ingenuity and I made out all right. When I got all the parts back where they were in the first place I looked around to see if I'd left anything out. Guess not. Now would be a good time for somebody to reassure me about the joys of year-round country life and the tedium of the fast city pace. I threw the switch. Well, things sucked wind and guzzled, but the gurgle was gone, and my ear at the intake suggested moisture. I went upstairs to push the button on the washing machine and there was some flow—enough, I thought, to do a cycle. I went to bed, the pump pumping and the washing machine trying. And the next morning, right after breakfast, I combed my hair and went to the order office of the mail order house, and I combed theirs. The girl said she couldn't imagine how such a mistake could even happen, and she said she was sorry. But she did have a repair kit for a Little Wonder, and I went home to take my pump apart again and fix it as good as new.

I agree that ours is certainly the good life. No water bills, no expensive plumbers, never cark nor care. The bowl of popcorn was flabby when I got to it, and it went to the hens. The hens, too, have a good life.

A Good One

As to what we do with our long winter evenings—my schedule isn't demanding, and I don't let them get that long. I like a glass of milk and a molasses cookie about ten minutes past eight, and by a quarter past eight I am usually on my way to knitting up my ravel'd sleeve of care. This concludes my program for the day and by breakfast time I am ready to rise and take new interest. Now and then something will interrupt this pleasant schedule, and were I to be asked for an example I might recall the night the fox snarled. I suppose not too many city folks have heard a fox snarl during a crisp Maine winter night with the moon full and high over the spruces and Peace snug under the blanket. Be it known, then, that a fox has two remarks. One is the yap, which sounds like any puppy dog's playful agreement with his environment and will never be uttered in anger. The yap of a fox is friendly and pleasant; I once watched a vixen playing with her young and now and then she would yap, at which the young ones would all yap back, and it was like a schoolmarm and her pupils playing scootchtag at recess.

But the snarl of a fox is another matter. It ranks with the hair-raising shrieks and screams uttered in ancient writings by supernatural fiends to cause people to lead better lives. The fox turns on his snarl when he is agitated about something. Perhaps surprised. Maybe a skunk stood up suddenly in his path. Maybe another fox got to the loose hen first. It could be he is

just venting his disrespect of mankind from the safety of a distant knoll. It happens we are well foxed in this precinct. There
are times when red fox fur is in demand and the hunters whit-
tle them down. Then, wildlife has cycles and when rabbits are
plentiful foxes are likewise; when rabbits decline so do the foxes.
But we keep having foxes enough. Here in Maine we've never
gone for the yoicks-away, tally-ho, John Peele sport of hunting
foxes, and I am glad. My neighbors would look silly riding
around in red coats. A Maine foxhunt calls for a good lunch
and a pleasant companion, and a hound to exercise the fox
while the hunters sit on two stumps and drink lunch. Sometimes the fox is beguiled into approaching close enough so the
hunters can get a shot off, and when the fox is missed he will
snarl. When a fox snarls under those conditions, he makes a
good one. It will make the earflaps on the hunters' caps stand
up.

So there was this beautiful winter night with the stars tingling at my window, and this fox sneaked up and stood right
there as if he owned the place. When food is hard to find a fox
will invade a dooryard like that. And I guess he was mad
because he didn't find anything to eat. So he let go with a
great-granddaddy snarl, starting the clapboards on the house
and attracting my attention. The next thing I knew, I was out
behind the barn in my bare feet, a shotgun with no shell in it
clutched in my shaking hands, and my lightweight sleeping
garment proving the season for same was over. As I began to
awake and found myself thus, I came to realize I had been
roused by the snarl of a fox. When I looked later, tracks in the
snow told me just how close the fox had been when he snarled,
and it was seven feet from him to me. I remembered nothing
of jumping from bed, descending the stairs, grabbing the gun,
and trotting around outdoors. Such is a snarl. The fox, by now,
was over in the next township and is useful to the narrative
only to show that a snarl is that kind of a noise. When I returned
into the house I opened the front damper in the stove, made
me a glass of warm milk, and by that time I was restored enough

so I put the shotgun back on its pegs. After I quieted down enough I went back to bed, but not to sleep. The thing about a fox snarl is that you lie awake wondering if the fool thing will do it again. He didn't, that night—and come to think of it, I haven't heard a fox snarl since then.

Ready to Go

The wheelbarrow has been shamefully neglected as a winter sport. Once or twice I have suggested it when some of our summertime friends reappear in the middle of the winter, bound for the ski slopes. I recommend the wheelbarrow as a much better way to exercise, but they've always gone skiing anyway. How well I remember the winter the wheelbarrow came to my attention as a fine excuse to get out into the exhilarating open air, to take the flabbiness out of tired muscles, to redeem the flagging spirits during the doldrums of the dull days! That year, as I painfully recall, my wheelbarrow had fulfilled its summer duties when I trundled in the last load of dry beans. I should have pushed it to the far end of the barn, tipping it up against the wall to hibernate, but I didn't and I have no idea why I didn't. I just supposed I had done so, and that come spring it would be right there in good shape and ready to go. So we had a rousing fine snowstorm one night, one to bring joy to all, and as I looked about the next morning I saw the wheelbarrow skulking at the corner of the house—right where I'd left it—full of snow and about three inches of each handle sticking out of the drift. I thought, of course, "Now, that's curious! How did that get out there?" Fact is, I said to my wheelbarrow, "What's going on?" There's nothing wrong, really, in speaking to a wheelbarrow.

It's when the wheelbarrow talks back that you want to sit down and think things over. And perhaps folks unaccustomed to the rural scene will not know what a wheelbarrow does, besides fill itself with snow, when it is left outdoors in the winter to fend for itself. It freezes itself to the ground at all three contact points—that's what it does.

Now, if you're paying attention, here I come—a fine, bronzed vision of a man, full of fun and longing to be well thought of, and I am eager to do the right thing. It is my purpose to retrieve the snow-laden wheelbarrow and put it in the barn where it should have been all the time. You notice that I approach the wheelbarrow and position myself between the handles, grasp them with both hands, lift, and push myself out through the bottoms of my socks in my boots. The wheelbarrow didn't move. There is a ripping sound of textiles gone awry, with a rending accompaniment as the muscles in my insteps, ankles, calves, thighs, hips, back, shoulders, and ears take up the slack. The wheelbarrow is *statu quo*. I realize a wheelbarrow full of snow isn't that heavy, so I conclude things are frozen down, and I go to find a shovel to dig and get a clear view of the problem. Now I fetch a pan of hot water and thaw the two legs and the wheel, and put the wheelbarrow in the barn. It has been a long time since I have had such a general physical workout, and it makes me feel good all over as I limp into the house. Nobody on any of Maine's ski slopes limps one bit better. Then I remembered that I'd forgotten to dump the snow out of the wheelbarrow, so I returned to the barn and did that. I didn't put the wheelbarrow away back, tipped against the wall, because other things were in the way and I didn't feel up to it.

When I came into the house I made remark on the great sport connected with pushing a wheelbarrow in deep snow, and after a short rest I was able to get my boots and socks off so I could have that beautiful relaxation which we call après-wheelbarrow. Then, the next morning, I found my wheelbarrow had moved again—it was now full of hay out by the mailbox, and when I went to get it I assumed it was frozen down again. It was not. I found this out when I exerted my strength to budge it and went up inside my hat. Inquiry revealed that the youngsters moved the wheelbarrow to get at the toboggan; the hay was an afterthought. They meant to stuff a grain bag with hay and make a cushion for the toboggan and were interrupted. Nobody knew why the bag couldn't have been filled with hay right in the barn. I creaked through February, but possibly what happened that next night added more exercise than I'd have had on a ski slope.

That next night I was recumbent with a mail order catalog that offered me a chance at one million dollars if I would buy sixteen white shirts for twenty-five dollars. I already had a white shirt somewhere, so I had to pass up this generous offer. Then I heard a hen squawk and left the house immediately with the supposition that a weasel was at the poultry. In this way I found my wheelbarrow was on the back steps waiting for me to come out. Riding a wheelbarrow takes considerable skill when you do it on purpose, but when the canter is a surprise to both you and the wheelbarrow, the need for concentrated coordination is intensified. I rode my wheelbarrow about forty yards, and then thinking I had gone far enough I gracefully alighted on one ear.

In the summertime, a wheelbarrow is useful and tries to keep its place. In the winter it affords good, healthy, invigorating sport, and seldom misses a chance.

Hardly in Touch

Boston, I heard on the radio, was about to have another practice alert, so people will know what to do when the bomb lands. I had just been to Boston that past week, urging my bankers to greater effort, so this forthcoming practice alert interested me more than it should have. Boston, to me, always looks as if something just let out, and I don't mix with it too well. It is bad enough, I say, to be in Boston when things are normal, and to be there during a bomb alert, even in practice, would tucker me. Well, I've never learned to run to get into an elevator. When I'm to Boston, and I have to take an elevator, the man always looks up to see me coming and begins to shut the door. But before he gets the door closed in my face, fifteen conditioned Bostonians will lope up at full tilt and get inside. I found out long ago that when an elevator goes up it always comes down again and there's always another trip. The same with the subway. Bostonians run for subway trains as if this is the last one forever.

It amused me on my trip to Boston to reflect that I ought to get some little cards printed, which I could pass out to people to explain why I am not running for elevators and subway trains. They might appreciate knowing why I seem to be so crazy amongst 'em. But I think they wouldn't understand why running for elevators makes anybody look lackin', to put it in a Maine way.

So I've been wondering what Boston will do when the whistle blows for keeps and everybody has to hightail it for safety—and perhaps escape up here to my relaxed sanctuary. When that happens, if I should chance to be in Boston, I think I would be in the way of a lot of people and would prove unpopular. During a bomb alert I would hesitate to pass out little cards and explain that I am only visiting. I'm thankful that so far the public safety program, the civil defense syndrome, has escaped me up here where I don't have to run for anything. I have found it is a good thing to live so far out of town that you can't hear any whistles. I am hardly in touch. I've considered the bomb, and have decided that if some foreign potentate wants to spend $5,000,000,000.00 to drop a nuclear bomb on me, it would be the biggest compliment in history. The end result, at least to me, would be no more than getting struck by lightning—a risk I take many times every summer without panic. I find a spritely pleasure in contemplating the cost of my extermination.

But if the plan is to exterminate Boston, my indifferent situation here might be useful. Assuming I survive, I might be handy enough to help if the Bostonians will slow down as they pass by. If I have provisions enough, I would share with needy folks fleeing from devastation, but I would like to have them approach in an orderly fashion. All of this will depend on whether or not the warden can blow his whistle before the bomb arrives, and the last Bostonian can catch the last bus as it pulls out.

(Disregard the foregoing if the bomb
falls before this book is published.)

A Good Story

Snow is relative. A couple of inches will paralyze Washington, D.C., but two feet at Seboomook Dam are just a light dusting. One winter a Great Northern Paper Company snowplow truck got stuck in a light dusting at Seboomook Dam, and it took two weeks to dig it out. The Great Northern figures one truck and two men to every hundred miles of wilderness road, a statistic the public works department in Washington, D.C., will consider inadequate, even though no snowplow has ever been stuck in a Washington snowbank for two weeks. The truth is that the State of Maine never gets enough snow in the long winter average to justify the expense of a trip to Florida, but it is also true that once in a while the long winter average blows up. When the same Great Northern has to extend another ten feet on the snow board at Lobster Lumber Camp, the sojourner in the sunny clime is getting his money's worth. Still, the Blizzard of Eighty-eight persists as a substantial disaster.

In my distinguished career as a dedicated addict to the horrors of a Maine winter, I truthfully remember but one occasion when things got bad enough so we didn't have to lie to make a good story for the summer folks. It was some years back. We had gone on some errand and the storm shut down while we were away from home. It was a northeaster, and it hit quick and fast, piled up snow, and kept at it until the afternoon the next day. The wind was diligent and plentiful. It was well after suppertime that we tooled our automobile off the numbered highway onto our own farm road. The thing shoved into a snowbank so the headlamps disappeared, and we sat there in the dark. Our house was a good half mile up the hill. Our conveyance was clearly beached for the duration, and I had some trouble forcing a door against the snow so we—wife, daughter, and I—could flounder through the drifts to a house not far away. Some other people who got stuck before we did were already there, but a couple of chairs were still available. Wife and daughter slept there sitting up that long night, but they were warm and out of the storm. I waded up the road and got home, taking care of the chores before I made myself a hot supper. The wind howled all night and was still howling when I got out of bed the next morning to look upon an obliterated world. I did the morning chores, and after breakfast got onto my snowshoes, and with a second pair tied to it I dragged the toboggan down the highway, approximately, to recover my marooned womenfolk. I got them home all right, but it was like scaling the polar icecap. Wife and I experienced snow blindness, but Daughter had great fun with a free ride on the toboggan.

The snow continued, and by now our kitchen windows were covered. To the front of the house, towards the road and where the northeast wind struck, there was bare ground—a fact of importance because from the front windows I could see to the highway. It happened we did not lose electric power in that storm, and not long after supper our telephone rang, so we were in contact. It was the highway commissioner. He wanted to know if I had seen a snowplow. I told him I had not, but would be glad to see what one looked like as soon as he could make arrangements. I told him when he came up the road to miss my automobile, which was in the middle. "The radio aerial is sticking up," I said.

He said things were in a mess. Most of his equipment had broken pinions, warped camshafts, moisture in the distributors, and other ailments brought on by too much snow. One truck was in the ditch on Summer Street, and he needed to find another truck to pull that one out and get it to plowing again. He thought there might be a truck up my way. He, himself, was at home, snowed in, and couldn't get out of his driveway. I said I'd watch for a truck, flag it down, relay the story. He said he'd appreciate that. He said he wished to hell he'd been smart and gone to Floridy.

I watched for a truck for a while, but none came, and I went to bed. And, once in bed, I heard a truck grinding away. I got to the front windows in time, toggled a light switch, and the truck blinked its headlamps in recognition. The ancient mug-up tradition still goes in these parts, so I headed for the kitchen to bring the pot to a boil and break out the pie. The driver and his spell-man came in, floundering and then stomping, and they said the road was filling in behind them as fast as they pushed it out in front. "This one's for the books!" the driver said. I told him he was wanted down on Summer Street to pull a snowplow out of the ditch, and he said, "Haw-haw!" We sat around and talked for a pie and a half and then they churned off down the road and I went back to bed. At daylight, our drifted highway showed no sign of the truck's having passed in the night, but the dirty dishes in the sink proved I hadn't dreampt it.

The snowplow crew came back two days later to have some more pie, and this time they left our road ready for travel. Now I could go and get my automobile, and we could go anywhere

94

we wished—even to Florida. But we didn't go anywhere. The storm was an experience, but not a bad one. The world was clean and white, spanking-shining new. The philosopher has told us that the Almighty who brings us snow will, in time, remove it, and He did, and He always has. We don't get real storms like that often, and certainly not every winter, and when we get one it wouldn't seem right to me to miss it.

A Fuller Flavor

There always comes a wonderful, warm spring day when nobody comes near me and I go to select the first parsnip for the vernal rites. Too bad some of our summer folks don't know about the Parsnip Party, or they'd come early enough to get in on it. But then, again—what about the bees? Bees are the reason nobody approaches and I am alone and unattended as I wend to last summer's garden and snare this year's parsnips.

All winter the bees have been snug in their hives with nothing to do but eat honey, survive, and look forward to spring. Bees don't hibernate, but stay active, although just barely. They move about in their hives during winter only enough to bring their clustered warmth over a new place on the combs, and by the time the first dandelion perks its yellow head they will have used most of their stores of honey. On Parsnip Day, which will be the first pleasantly warm day of the unfolding year, a day we can safely assume considerable frost has left the ground, the bees will rouse as the morning sun caresses the front of their hive, and they will burst forth for their first flight of the season. Burst, indeed—they come out in great exuberance until the air nearby is full of them, hundreds of thousands of bees all hither and thither amongst themselves, wheeling, dipping, veering, turning, criss-crossing. To the beekeeper, this is a stirring sight, and sound, for it proves his bees have wintered and will be ready for the approaching honey flow. The sound is a vibrant hum, loud enough to close out other sounds, as when somebody calls to me from the house. All right, so this first springtime flight is properly called the "cleansing flight." The bees have been within the hive ever since the last aster bloomed last fall, and to put it discreetly, there are no water closets in a beehive. The bees have been saving up. And when they fly on this happy occasion they cleanse themselves as they go, hit or miss. It is a unanimous defecation, simultaneous and concomitant. If, as is often the case, the housewife has chosen this fine spring day to hang some sheets on the washline, all white and lovely, she will not be glad.

It usually happens that this day of the cleansing flight is still coolish around the edges, and some of the bees will disport beyond the warmth. In the shadow somewhere, and a bee will take a chill and not be able to fly back into the sunlight and to the hive. Life in a beehive is cheap, and a few lost stragglers won't matter, but the bee who feels a chill will respond to a helping hand, so to speak, and I like to offer one. Understand that during these cleansing flights the bees are happy and care-free. They exult. Hooray, it's spring, and let's cavort! Since no honeybee ever stings except in defense of the hive or the queen, a beekeeper never fears one in the field, and on cleansing day in particular there is no chance of a sting. All the bees are too happy, in love with the new year. So it is fun to stand there where the bees are enacting this ceremony and hold out a hand, palm up. A cool bee, sensing the warmth of a human hand, will settle down—and there you are taking part in this celebration with a half-dozen cool bees on your hand. They sit there fretting their wings, murmuring gratitude for their comfort. After a moment a cool bee will regain his thermal needs and take off, rejoining the flight and eventually returning to the hive.

There was a Parsnip Morning I sensed that the bees would appear, so I suggested the laundry be skipped, and about ten o'clock the fun began. Out they came, and it was to be one of the pleasantest cleansing flights since Vergil wrote his *Eclogues*. I was standing under a grapevine arbor, shielded from the impending bee dung, and over my shoulder I saw an automobile come into the yard. Man got out. Stranger to me. Looked like a salesman; he had a satchel. He thumped on the house door and I was pointed out to him. Down he came, eager with his business. I bade him a pleasant good morning, and he opened his satchel to show me a pair of shoes. No living person, he said, had ever been confronted with a greater opportunity than now lay before me. He asked me what size I wore. They certainly were fine-looking shoes, and I began wrestling with my ingrown sales resistance. But then I reached out my hand, and I got six bees all at once. Meantime, about three hundred and fifty other bees had found this salesman and were flying about the end of his nose to show their appreciation. In this way his attention was called to the cleansing flight.

"Bees," I said. "Cleansing flight! Great show!"

But the salesman was gone. So my observations of the cleansing flights have always been by myself. I have nobody to talk to, and this is too bad because I might talk about parsnips. Things in nature act and react. The bees have nothing to do with parsnips, and parsnips with bees. It's just that the first day of warmth that will send forth the pent-up bee is also far enough along so a parsnip can be dug. Parsnips grow the previous summer, and need to "winter over" to attain a fuller flavor. Spending the winter in the frozen ground gives them character. The flight of the bees merely tells me that today I can harvest a parsnip. Which, after I attend the flight, I do.

And the people who wouldn't stand around in a flight of bees will have to take my word for parsnips. I like to parboil my first parsnips maybe half an hour, and while this is going on I fry up a goodly snatch of bacon. Bacon goes well with fried parsnips. I now have a decent splash of bacon fat in my frypan. Now I lay strips of my parboiled parsnips on a platter, sprinkle them with some yellow cornmeal, and anoint them with a sufficiency of granulated maple sugar—I had prepared the sugar during maple season just previously with parsnips in mind. Now the parsnips are ready for the bacon fat, which should be vice versa, and I have only to remember to break in a couple of eggs to piecen out. And you take a feed of new fried parsnips with with-its, and you'll understand why the cleansing flight of the bees is something to look forward to.

Coming Along Nicely

Of the many things that engage our rural attention during the winter, some are more important than others, but important or not we do not sit and twiddle our thumbs in idle disinterest. I, at least, keep intellectually active to an astonishing degree—sometimes giving much thought to small topics nobody in the cities ever bothers with. For instance, who has given the slightest thought to a story in the papers that says the Federal Security Administration has granted $19,000 a year to Cornell University to do research on "tolerance for environmental stress in aged and newborn sheep and goats"? I suspect urban people didn't even read the story. Too bad, because everybody should be interested that the Cornell researchists are coming along nicely and will render a full report soon.

Had I known about this grant in its earlier research, I would have hurried to tell the Cornell professors that a newborn sheep can be tolerated without too much trouble, but some of the older ones do require some adjustment. An elderly male sheep is best tolerated at considerable distance. I have a neighbor down the road about a mile who has an aged sheep, and at that distance I am able to tolerate him fairly well. However, an aged goat is another matter, and a mile or two one way or the other doesn't make all that much difference. An aged goat, even when he is engaged in the most introspective meditation and is plainly alone with his thoughts, has a way of making his presence known, and this calls for a great deal of tolerance by everybody. I recall one aged goat of the neighborhood that used to get loose once in a while, and because of excessive environmental stress he used to wander off and think he was lost. It is difficult to lose an aged goat. Even if the wind shifts and blows hard, the stress on the environment leaves the whereabouts of the goat about the same, whether he's loose or tied.

As I meditated on this, whiling away an afternoon, I didn't dwell wholly on sheep and goats. I began to feel good about Congress. If I thought for one minute that my congressman was indifferent about tolerating aged sheep and goats, I would withdraw my support and write him a letter. We needn't worry about the Ship of State so long as we have a Congress that is sensitive to the tolerance of aged sheep and goats. And we needn't worry about the excellence of our educational system so long as we have such generous grants to institutions like Cornell. I'm just glad Congress doesn't spend all our money on frivolities like foreign relations and domestic needs.

I hope Cornell is also studying the tolerance of goats after old age and when one ceases to be. Considerable tolerance is needed when an aged goat is processed, reincarnated, and rises resplendent in the butcher shop with a sign on him that says, "Lamb Fores." Maybe the $19,000 granted to Cornell isn't enough. The great question of what becomes of aged goats needs all the tolerance it can get.

Now and then we have a chance to watch with great amusement these former city people who have retired to start a new life. They acquire five acres of nature's honest earth, where they will live in independent happiness. They cultivate angleworms and lay out herb gardens, planning to retail little bunches of fennel and marjoram. They will keep a hive of bees, and they will knit their own underwear from the wool of a sheep

that will graze on bushes and cost them nothing. These people are always organic, and take the magazine and put up the sign. Then they write their book, and one chapter always tells how they gain their sustenance from their mini-garden and the milk of a goat they keep on the back porch. And anybody who does his best thinking during the complacency of a Maine winter is glad to know that. Five acres aren't enough for a goat. If I had a goat, I would keep him in Montana, and I could tolerate him as long as I stayed in Maine. All keepers of goats, I notice, arrive at the same conclusion, sooner or later. They put out a roadside sign that says, "Goat for Sale." Let somebody else tolerate the thing for a while.

Bumbling Through

You can have a lot of good, country-evening fun with all the stories about how food got invented. Almost any magazine you pick up will bring out something or other, usually about Kate. Kate was the dumb Indian maiden (stock character No. 4) who was always trying to cook something in the kitchen and always came up with something else. Well, here's the story about the invention of the potato chip, vouched for by a firm in Saratoga, New York, which makes potato chips. Kate was frying off a batch of doughnuts one time and somehow let a bit of potato fall into the hot fat. Something about this magazine piece makes me think Kate was not doing this back in the days of wampum and tepees and scalping exercises, but was now somewhat civilized and was a short-order cook in a restaurant. It would be late in her distinguished career, when she was maybe a hundred and eighty-five years old. Kate tasted this shred of potato and found it good. She showed her boss, and he immediately set up the Saratoga Potato Chip Company.

Bless good Kate! At that time she had already invented red flannel hash, succotash, doughboys, filled cookies, deep dish apple pie, tarts, turnovers, Tollhouse cookies, and the hot cross bun—all by accident. The world is indebted to Kate for everything good to eat. She was a blundering kitchen hand who couldn't start any kind of cookstove task without winding up out in left field with a new taste sensation. She invented Shredded Wheat while stuffing sausage, invented spaghetti and meatballs while trimming a mince pie, invented cole slaw while stewing prunes, and came up every day with something better than she was making. Interesting that Kate invented the banana fritter while roasting a duck—seventy-five years before the banana was introduced into this country. The devotion of the magazines to Kate is amazing. The whole history of cookstove innovation comes via Kate, by any other name, who never quite brought anything off without a side order of something else. Womenkind in general, as the heritage custodians of kitchen accomplishment, never produced a thing—only Kate.

Mankind in general, meaning us gents, never worked that way. We invented the reaper because we needed a reaper. It was not produced as an afterthought while somebody was shingling a barn. The man said to himself, "We need a reaper," and he went ahead and produced a reaper. But nothing in the food line was ever produced in that simple, straightforward way. No woman ever paused in her kitchen to say, "Now, what we ought to have is a strawberry shortcake!" and then went ahead to make one. Instead, she left everything to Kate, who invented the strawberry shortcake one day while she was cooking some creamed onions. Again, her employer tried the mistake, liked it, and had it enacted. Now, I have a cookbook written in French and translated into English in 1804, and it tells how to make potato chips and how to serve them. There isn't one word in either language about Kate and how she is going to invent potato chips in 1853, while working in Saratoga.

The magazines are a little confused about Kate and the potato chip, because the pot of hot fat for frying doughnuts is quite another story. There is more doughnut lore than there is law about line fences, and some of it does include Kate. The story about Kate and doughnuts was written in Penobscot picture language on birch bark and was long hidden in an oak tree in Connecticut. It says that one day she was deep-frying some hush-puppies to go with a porcupine stew. (You may recall that Kate invented hush-puppies while grilling some lamb chops in Tucson, Arizona, in 1849.) It seems Kate's boyfriend had been warned off the premises by Kate's stern father, Chief Stand-on-a-stump-in-the-rain, so the boy attempted to send Kate a love letter attached to an arrow. The arrow plunked into the kettle of hot fat, piercing a hush-puppy and leaving in it a great gaping hole. The fat caught fire and burned the place down, but Kate miraculously made her escape, clutching the wounded hush-puppy in her hand. As she came out, she was exclaiming, "Oh, do not do that! Oh, do not do that!" and thus the do-not, or doughnut, was born.

But in quite another story, Kate was cook and chambermaid on a barkentine out of Camden, Maine (some say North Windham), and one day while making seagull goulash, on which the captain doted, she accidentally got a dumpling stuck on the lily iron she was using to stir the pot. Upon finding this punctured dumpling on his plate, the captain cried out in glee, "Oh, what a splendid dainty to thrust on the spoke of the wheel whilst I am holding *Rebecca* on course and betimes need a lunch!" (*Rebecca* was the name of the barkentine, in memory of a school teacher in Framingham, Massachusetts.) When the captain asked Kate what she called this dumpling with a hole in it, she answered in Penobscot (she was never proficient in English), "Higmut, hogmut, me not mutt mutt," which means, "When the sky is pink in the morning, the woodchuck is pink, too." The captain thought she said doughnut, and thus the doughnut was born. After that, Kate kept a pride of doughnuts and the captain sailed all over the world with the doughnuts stuck on the spokes of his steering wheel, munching as he sailed, in fair weather and foul. This story has credence in a number of places it will be polite not to identify. Well, the story suffers from a few things. One is that Maine sea captains never steered their own boats, but had a hand who was called the *wheelman*. Another is that Kate, at the time, was in Saratoga inventing the potato chip. Also, the *Rebecca* didn't have a steering wheel, but was handled by a tiller. (Although the museum at Camden does have a considerable collection of doughnut holes to bolster the steering-wheel story, some of which went around The Horn numerous times.)

But the thing to remember is that nothing fit to eat was ever produced with malice aforethought and brought to table by some woman who planned on it. It was always Kate, bumbling through. She invented maple syrup by accident—also dill pickles, peanut brittle, and Betty Crocker. She stupidly baked two half-pound cakes together and invented the pound cake. She invented whipped cream and scrambled eggs. Lemon meringue was a by-product of cottage cheese, and she invented fried onion rings while baking an Alaskan—he had been half baked before that. Who will ever forget how she invented gingerbread while singe-ing a hen? We owe the girl a great deal. Without Kate, the world would still be eating plain food.

Not Sold in Stores

One dandy way to get away from a rugged Maine winter is to have a woodworking shop, like mine, with a lit-tle stove that uses the scrap lumber and weaves the magic of comfort for self and friends while the north wind doth blow and poor Robin is in Guatemala. Here, I make things or I do not make things, and sometimes the neighbors bring me things to fix, and one day it is time to start the celery seeds. But my shop is not at all like those you see in the hobby magazine advertisements—they are always so neat. Here is one picture that I cut out to tack to the wall. It shows jubilant Daddy about to bore a ⅜th-inch hole in the gable of a new doghouse, using an electric drill that is the reason for the advertisement, while Mommy sits nearby on a stool, beaming joy, and Sonny-boy leans closer to get a good look. A delightful family scene.

The big trouble is that the advertisement has its emphasis on the drill at the expense of accuracy. It looks to me as if the drill is going to cut through the ¼-inch plywood like a hot knife through butter, and the boy is about to be given the same treatment—if he isn't killed he's going to be scairt into a decline from which he will recover only after many years. The drill is a beautiful thing, and so is Mother, but in less than three seconds Mother is going to jump eight feet in the air and accuse poor old stupid Daddy of trying to kill their firstborn.

My shop goes along otherwise, advertising notwithstanding. When my wife, also good-looking, first stepped into my shop as a fetching bride, she fell over a dewheeled bicycle into a basket of ripe tomatoes, and when I turned to see what made all the clamor I beaned her with a plank. This left her cool about shops and if she comes now in the serenity of experience she thumps on the door with a broom handle and shouts from outside. I think she hasn't been inside my shop in forty-five years.

The boy, our boy, on the other hand, became chummy as soon as he could hit a nail, and soon learned enough about tools so he doesn't hang around while Daddy is boring a hole. This advertisement, if it meant to tell the truth about shops, would have Mommy poised in a warning shriek that would back Junior up against the far wall. Also, the shop wouldn't be so neat. After making a doghouse, any home-workshop buff will have shavings and sawdust aplenty, and a Band-Aid on at least one thumb. And the tools, you bet, will not be so methodically arranged. I never found any way to keep a proper son from moving tools around. I have an adequate assortment of chisels and slicers and racks to hold them, but when I want a chisel I seldom step forthrightly to pick one down. I find it's quicker to go into the house and shout, "Anybody know where I can find a chisel?" Sometimes anybody does, and sometimes anybody does not. Chisels outside of magazine advertisements are usually accounted for thus:

1. In the kitchen, borrowed to decap a pickle jar.
2. In the 4-H chicken pen, where a window stuck.
3. Down cellar, where a screw was loose in the Ping-Pong table.

4. In the drawer for bits and drills. (The bits are with the sandpaper, the drills are in the spice closet in the pantry, and
   the rack for chisels is full of files.)

This doesn't mean that my shop is disorganized.

It is as well organized as can be reasonably arranged outside
of a hobby magazine. I do have all the tools the magazines suggest, plus some I think they never heard of—pod-augers, cob-
bler's leather trimmers, some farrier's fleams, a harness vice,
mowing knife grinder, some stone-splitting tamps. And, my shop
is much more than a simple hobby nook. It handles household
repairs not only for ourselves but for the neighborhood, and
beyond. It becomes a factory for pretties when I stoke the stove
in the deep of winter and make things not sold in stores. My
silver chests are handsome, and I've been known to build a boat.
Most of all, maybe, my shop is a haven for the oppressed and
weary, who come in to stomp snow off their feet, bringing the
woes of the world to warm them by my fire—and which we
quickly settle for the good of mankind without charge. But none
of this, that, these, and those is done without making sawdust
and shavings that would show up in a picture, and without some
clutter and misplacement. I am not unneat, and I frequently tidy
up. Sometimes I sweep. And I do try to keep tools in their places.
But the function of a shop is to absorb and accommodate whatever takes place in it, and the magazines don't always know
about that. I think the word is verisimilitude.

There was another picture I cut out that showed a happy hob-
byist who had spent the winter making birdhouses. There he
stood, surrounded by birdhouses, smiling for the camera. Had
there been verisimilitude, he would have been standing hip deep
in shavings—enough to truck to a pulpmill and get paid. But
there wasn't a shaving in sight. Among the birdhouses, his chisel
rack was neat and orderly, every chisel arranged by size, as trim
as the teeth on a comb. Only trouble was that his chisel rack was
under a shelf of paint cans, so close that there was no way to lift
one of the chisels out of its slot. Smilingly, like Tom Swift, I

wrote to the magazine and asked about the shavings, and how he got to use any of his chisels. The editor was kind enough to reply, and he said possibly the man had swept up to please the photographer, but he had no idea about the chisels. Which didn't assuage my curiosity, but which perhaps explains magazine pictures. Meantime, I like my shop just the way it is, and it's a great place to spend the winter.

Necktie and All

"Who invented the electric cable?" demanded Daughter Kathy one evening some time ago as she dumped her school books in my lap as if they had failed her. I had heard the school bus churning up the road through the new snow, so I wasn't astonished to see her. Her question seemed to me to be a good one, and just about on her par for evening homecoming, so I went along with it and I said, "Let me have three guesses—Mr. Pratt?"

"Who is Mr. Pratt?" she asked.

I said, "There are several of them. One is Percy Pratt. He's secretary of the chamber of commerce over in Freeport."

"Did he invent the electric cable?"

"I don't think so," I said. "Next time I see him I'll inquire."

"Oh, Daddy!"

I give the details to show to what lengths I went sometimes to advance the education of my children, but also to show that the lean days of the cooler months give us Mainers a chance to enhance our own erudition and add to our intellectual capacities. Kathy's question was overstated. She wasn't after the inventor of the electric cable, who was not Percy Pratt, but she was seeking the story of the laying of the Atlantic cable. After we had bantered pleasantly, I helped her with what we had available in our household books, so we came up with Cyrus Field and everything she needed for her classwork. I promised that when the weather would be more amiable I'd drive her to Portland and she could stand up in Fort Allen Park and look down at the remains of the wharf where the steamship *Great Eastern* was tied up while she was in port during the laying of the cable. When we had the Atlantic cable in hand, Kathy said, "All right, but if Teacher asks me, who *did* invent the electric cable?" I did the best I could. I rambled about Samuel F. B. Morse, whom Field consulted, and how the little relay dinguses that perked up a fading impulse were the whole secret of long-distance telegraphy. We did a few dots and dashes, too. Turned out the teacher didn't ask.

Well, the next day, being a Tuesday, I was at the shop window thinking how much I have to know to keep a daughter on the honor roll, and trying to find a washer that would suit my need, and I saw an automobile arrive in our dooryard. A man got out and went to ring our front door bell. Our front door bell rings all right if you push the button, but nobody pays any attention. The normal presumption will be that somebody is trying to be funny. The way to get into our house has always been to open the back door and yell, "Hi-hi!" This man persisted at the front door button for some time, and from the shop I could hear the bell in the kitchen ringing its heart out. I knew my wife was sitting in the kitchen rocker reading Alcibiades and chuckling to herself as she thought I was playfully tingling and would have a wisecrack if she was nutty enough to respond. The whole thing was amusing, and just as I found the washer I needed I heard the man thumping at the back door. Now he came into my shop, and he was a fine-looking specimen. Well dressed, necktie and all. Shoes shined. He shook my hand with enough energy to hoe a row of beans, and inquired pleasantly if I might be Kathy's father. I told him I was often accused of that, and I asked him what I could do to make his happiness complete. I thought I detected a suspicion of doubt in this gentleman's mind that anybody so simple as I could have sired a paragon, and this caused me to say, "I think perhaps you're going to try to sell me something?"

It was even so. This man had rented a booth at Topsham Fair, and as the young folks attending this exposition had passed he was able to get their names and addresses—on the middle day of Topsham Fair our schools always had holiday so all the youngsters could go. Now he was calling on all the parents, and this would keep him busy all winter. He said that since I was Kathy's father, I was naturally concerned that she should gain in wisdom and understanding, and he was selling the finest of all encyclopedias—the Mammoth, Mastodon, Nix Plus Ultra, all-inclusive and complete twenty-four-volume masterpiece of the Universe Publishing Corporation. He opened his case and revealed this marvel. Certainly, he said, with a daughter so alert and talented as Kathy I would be eager to invest in her future. The man was now well into his set sales pitch, and I was thinking of Kathy, one day a useful woman, well rounded and able to converse lucidly on all subjects, the pride of her parents. I heard the man say his comprehensive compendium had been approved by all leading educators.

"Who approved the educators?" I asked.

"A panel of unbiased scholars!" he said, and he whipped out a brochure and showed me the faces of these unbiased scholars. He pointed to their names, and their biographies.

"Never knew we had so many!" I said.

All right. Were I to buy a book, or a set of books, I would wend to a bookstore and do so. Dooryard salesmen, even if they were to have something I wanted, find me penniless. I was about to say this to the man, which would bring our colloquy to an end, when he said, "You will find these books of vast value to yourself as well—you can be ready to answer questions. You wouldn't want to have Kathy ask a question you couldn't answer . . ."

So I said, "All right—who invented the electric cable?"

He said, "Who invented the electric cable?"

"Yes," I said. "Who invented the electric cable—Kathy asked me that last night."

"So," he said, "you well know what I mean. How important it is to be ready with accurate information! Here—this volume has the E's—we'll just run down a few pages. Let me see, now—electric . . ."

I went to put the washer on whatever it was I wanted a washer for, and when I came back he had his books spread around the shop. I went down cellar to fill a vinegar jug, and he was still looking when I came up. But he went away after a while. That night I admonished Kathy about dallying with the names of her mother and father in the presence of book salesmen, thus advancing her education a good deal. And if, I said, the teacher asks about the electric cable again, it will be all right to mention Percy Pratt. "Tell her," I said, "that you have it on the authority of an unbiased scholar."

Watching Turtles

It was being a forlorn winter evening and I was wondering about my friends down south when the television brought joy—it showed a tank full of turtles swimming about, and each turtle had a watch strapped around his middle. This was to inform me that I could buy a watch that wouldn't leak for under $20.00—but it also made me wonder why a turtle needs to know what time it is. Then I thought a turtle probably doesn't care any more than I do, except that I don't carry a watch. That's true. I never have carried a watch. And it's not because I don't have one; I have two very fine watches. They are in my bureau drawer and they have been there for more than fifty years. They run if I wind them, and they'll keep time. Both are family hand-me-downs—one from Great-Uncle Levi who homesteaded a ranch in North Dakota, and one from Uncle Eddie who was chief bookbinder for T. B. Mosher.

That was Thomas Bird Mosher, considered the best of his trade. A book bound by T. B. Mosher in Portland, Maine, was a work of art. Uncle Eddie went with him as a boy apprentice, and by 1919 was his bindery foreman.

Uncle Levi left Maine soon after the Civil War, and after living seven years on a god-forsaken quarter section where Bismarck is now the capital of North Dakota, he took title and immediately sold out. During those seven years, required by the Homestead Act for gaining ownership, he learned that North Dakota is no place for a Maine Yankee, but he did bring back "east" with him enough stories to beguile three generations of nephews and nieces. When Levi had left home to go "out west," folks bidding him goodbye chipped in to buy him a fine watch to remember them by. It was a huge gold Hamilton that bore on its face, "R. L. Whitney, Lisbon Falls, Maine." Rolvin Whitney had been a boyhood chum of Levi, and instead of subscribing to the "fever" that took so many Maine boys to the prairies, he stayed at home and opened a bicycle shop on Main Street. Out back he greased sprockets and mended saddles, and an enterprising salesman had fixed him up with a consignment of watches to fill the front window on the sidewalk. Whether or not Rolvin ever actually sold a watch on a forthright customer-proprietor basis is not known, but this time he took whatever money had been donated and let Levi's friends have a watch. "at cost." It would be years before Levi had money to acquire a chain for his watch—a gold chain that reached across his belly with a pocket knife in the opposite vest pocket. And some years after that before he sported the "charm" in the middle with the Masonic emblem on one side and that of the Odd Fellows on the other.

Uncle Eddie's watch was—is—silver. When Eddie was a small

boy he was walking along Congress Street in Portland with his sister, playing wish-I-had with things in the store windows. In a jewelry window was a display of charms and fobs for watches, and one was an oxidized silver bulldog. Uncle Eddie said he wished he had that one, there, and he pointed at the silver bulldog. His sister didn't play wish-I-had in that window, because such fobs and charms were for men. But she remembered, and quite a few years later she had saved enough money to buy a silver bulldog watch charm for her brother. So he had a "watch" dog, but no watch. And just the opposite prevailed—it would be years before Uncle Eddie bought a watch, and years before Uncle Levi bought a chain.

As a bookbinder for T. B. Mosher, Uncle Eddie earned good money as long as he lived. But his life was short. Those were the days of "galloping consumption," and the old doc who looked Eddie over shook his head and suggested another climate. Eddie left Maine seeking such, and on his way he paused in Philadelphia to go into the store of Bailey, Banks & Biddle to buy a watch. He laid his silver bulldog on the counter and said he'd like a watch to go with it. And a chain. The clerk sold him a Longines, thinner and smaller than Uncle Levi's turnip of a Hamilton, and probably a good deal more expensive. Bailey, Banks & Biddle, yes—but you wouldn't expect class in a bicycle shop.

Uncle Levi's watch is one of those magnificent timepieces that railroad conductors used to affect. Does anybody remember how the railroad conductor would pull out his big Hamilton, stare at the face, move his lips as he counted seconds, and then catch a milepost out the train window? Trains didn't always run on time and the milepost could have been an hour late, but a conductor's watch was a convincing thing. I was riding one time on the grand old Louisville & Nashville and it was clear we'd be at least two hours late into Evansville. "When will we get to Evansville?" I asked the conductor.

He braced himself by my seat, looked up and down the car to see if things were tranquil enough so he might dally with

me, pulled out his great watch, held it off to accommodate his farsightedness. He studied it. He moved his lips with the second hand. Then he put the watch back in his pocket and said, "Pretty soon, now." I didn't tell him that he made me think of my Uncle Levi.

Uncle Levi lived a life in which fleeting time was not geared to his watch. His watch was on the shelf most of his seven years in Dakota. Then he worked for the Union Pacific Railroad, stoning up wells that would supply water to steam locomotives across Montana. The track crews would lay a siding where a well was to be and a well would be dug. Then Uncle Levi would come with a flatcar of rocks, mortar materials, a helper, and supplies. After pitching a tent, time was relative— Uncle Levi and his "cowan" weren't going anywhere until the well was stoned, and then only to the next well. Then he went to Colorado to prospect and he didn't need a watch for that. After that, he combed the Badlands, gathering Indian relics that he shipped, at a profit, to a dealer in New York. Here, again, it wasn't essential that he know quarter-past from quarter-to, so his watch was in the keeping of a friend in Bismarck. The Badlands had long been the burial place for the Sioux, and in this pursuit Uncle Levi made many friends among that Nation, and was accordingly spared some of the unkind activity of the times. When Chief Sitting Bull was finally captured and brought into Bismarck as a prisoner of the United States Cavalry, Uncle Levi was there in the crowd and they greeted each other as old friends—which they were. So, after many years Uncle Levi came home to Maine and brought his watch with him.

Uncle Eddie never did come home. After his pause in Philadelphia to buy a watch, he moved along somewhat as "tramp printers" did in those days. Anybody who could bind books for T. B. Mosher would have no trouble finding work as long as he could find a book binder, so Uncle Eddie would present himself, work for a while, and then move along as his illness progressed. He never did find a climate that helped him, and he never did really need a watch. What time was it for him?

Still a young man, Uncle Eddie's troubles were over. "A blessing!" they said. He came home in his casket, to be buried in the village cemetery at Gray Corner—and it would be many years before his mother would join him there. With him came two trunks—he had prudently made arrangements. In one of the trunks was his watch. And his silver bulldog with its silver chain.

So there was a forlorn winter evening when I might have sat around wondering about my friends down south. But the television showed a tank of turtles swimming with their watches, and after I turned the television off I pleasantly relaxed and thought on Uncle Levi and Uncle Eddie. I have no idea what time it was. On the way to bed I checked the bureau drawer, and Uncle Levi said 7:46:22. Uncle Eddie said 1:38:30.

That's what they said the last time I looked, and I expect they'll say the same next time.

She Wouldn't Move

The folks who leave us in September accordingly miss the spirited fun of the Maine gunning season, which opens in October. First comes the bird season, which is observed diligently in all vicinities, and there was one time I came within a hair's breadth of getting shot for a pa'tridge. I had foolishly failed to notice that September had lapsed over into October, and had forgotten to get down my scarlet hat and wear it indoors and out until the threat was over. Had I been shot that time, it would have been my own fault, because if you've got a red hat on and get shot, it is the hunter's fault. At the time, I was working on a new cover for my well—a bubbling source off the sidehill that is piped to the house.

The spring had been stoned up in my grandfather's day, but time intervened and now it needed a new cement cover. I had cast the cover, with a ring in it so we could lift it on and off if need be, and now I wanted to point up the stones around the top to make everything tight so the cover would seat evenly when it was lowered on. No great job, but I was down inside the spring, standing on a plank at water's level, swinging a trowel from a bucket of mortar. There is an aloneness about being down a well. The damp stones encircle you so there is nothing to see except damp stones, unless you look up. It must be a lot like being in a tomb. Light does come down, but it is a subdued light. No sound comes down. If there is wind, or a breeze, it penetrates not. I was alone and found that talking to myself was small entertainment. Well, in a henhouse, shed, shop, there is a forensic quality that inspires me to wise words, but down a well the most profound remarks fail to rebound. The only proof I had that the world above continued to function was the occasional shadow of Gelert, our dog, who would look in now and then to see if I were still there. But then there was no shadow of Gelert, and I assumed he had withdrawn to snooze and await my resurrection. It was when I had exhausted my pail of mortar that I came up my short ladder, like Aeneas, to retrace my steps and regain the outer air.

It was, in fact, the first day of October, and Maine has perhaps never had a more magnificent October first. The sky was high and blue, and from the coolth of the spring I adjusted pleasantly to the warmth of the upper day. Then I saw a dog. It was not Gelert, but was a stranger to me. She was a beautiful dog—a red setter, and she had me in a trancelike point. There is nothing of flesh and blood so like the marble of a statue as a red setter in a trancelike point. Gelert, who had been asleep (as I surmised), roused to discover this lady dog just as I came out of the ground. Gelert was a lady's man, and he was delighted. Gelert tried to

disengage the lady's attention, but a red setter in a trancelike point is not easy to disengage. She stood there with a front paw in the air, her head forward, her eyes on me, and her tail like a ramrod. Until I was flushed and flew up, she wouldn't move. Good dog! Gelert sat down and cocked his head to consider things. One of the great joys of a Maine October is to discover that somebody's bird dog thinks you are a pa'tridge. Over the dog's motionless shoulder I could see her master stealthily coming my way, fowling piece at the ready. He was clearly short-sighted, and I could see that he wasn't about to shoot me until he was close enough to be sure. All he wanted me to do was fly.

So I called a cheerful what-ho at him, supposing that a good way to save my life, and I saw at once that he was much astonished to learn that a pa'tridge can speak English. But he soon recovered and said it was a lovely day, an observation with which I concurred, and explained that he had taken advantage of the pleasant weather to get out and do a little hunting. His dog remained at a fine point, and Gelert continued to admire her. The four of us, dogs and men, stood thus for a moment or two, and then the man pulled a little whistle from his L. L. Bean jacket and blew on it vigorously. But it was an L. L. Bean dog whistle—the kind dogs can hear but humans can't. His dog paid no attention to the whistle and continued to point me, expecting me to fly up any minute, but Gelert, who had never heard an L. L. Bean dog whistle before, took a fright and ran into the woods and was gone for four days. Anything that made a noise except food falling in his dish always frightened Gelert.

The hunter then felt his way along warily, foot by foot, and tried to find his dog with his free hand. "Fine-looking dog," I said. The man was wearing lovely olive-green bird-hunting jacket and pants, a blaze-orange vest with game pockets, belt for his ax, ammunition, and utility cord, and I'd say his boots stood him sixty dollars. Down his front and on his red hat were fish-and-game-club emblems—things like crossed guns and fly rods, moose and bobcats, and the wary, wayfaring mallard. "Don't fall in the well," I said.

And thus, in some such idyllic manner, the Mainer usually

learns that September has waned, October has waxed, and it's time to break out the scarlet hat and practice ducking. It is the time of year when the Mainer, if pointed, is expected to fly. I suggested to this gentleman that he work his dog down along the stone wall towards the swamp. He thanked me, and with a fresh bucket of mortar I went back down in the well. One year I got three such hunters lost in the swamp. Then I got out my red hat, which has saved my life many times.

A Plastics Pioneer

In my continuing program of having something to do in the workshop to relax me during the long Maine winter, there was the time I made some cold-frame sash and thus encountered the vast amusement of being a pioneer in the new age of plastics. Time was we used glass for cold frames, but the glass people priced us, and themselves, out of that. This time, I foresaw a fortune in early cucumbers, and decided to put together a dozen or so cold frames for starting cucumber seeds before the season was ready for them. Well, in Maine the prudent gardener gets everything else planted and holds off his cucumbers until last. The fifteenth of June is about right—by that time the ground is warm enough for cucumbers, and the bugs will have gone their cycle by the time the plants are up. It was my notion to start a batch of cucumbers under cover and have them ready to set in the ground by June fifteenth, and thus beat the competition to the market. It worked, too, but while the frost was still in the ground I became a plastics pioneer.

When I got the wooden frames made, instead of going for glass, I sent away for a new product just devised by, let us say, Corporation A. The story in the farm magazine gave this new product a fine approval. Known as Transpeek, this clear plastic permitted the penetration of valuable sun rays that glass excluded. It was just dandy for plants. It was much cheaper than glass, and it wouldn't shatter if you dropped it. It was going to revolutionize the whole hothouse business. I was filled with desire.

We now bid adieu to prologue, and step into the brisk action of the play itself. We are about to get a clear view of American Industry at its very best—at top efficiency, at peak ability. Progress is our motto! "Better living through chemistry," and that sort of thing. Corporation A is man's leading benefactor. I wrote to Corporation A, inquiring about this marvelous new product and begging their attention. Corporation A replied immediately, thanking me for my interest, assuring me of their appreciation, and saying I had indeed made a wise choice. However, at this time they were unable to serve me, since they merely made Transpeek and had no facilities for supplying the consumer. Transpeek was of such recent development that a sales organization had not yet been effected, but if I would be patient I would receive further information shortly. They suggested I write to Corporation B, which would be the distributor for the building trades, and to Corporation C, which would handle the agricultural and horticultural markets for Corporation B. Thanking me again, they begged to remain mine truly.

Corporation A did enclose some "literature," which painted a rosy picture for Transpeek, and immediately I got the same printed matter from Corporations B and C. But Corporation B didn't send me any Transpeek and didn't tell me where I could get any. Corporation C was more helpful. They telephoned me from their New York office, affably welcoming me to their growing list of customers, and explained that they had not yet arranged for retail outlets in my vicinity. This was why they had used the telephone to get to me directly. I got the idea the man thought I was about to order at least ten carloads of Transpeek. I told him that through none of my doing the matter seemed out of hand. I said I wouldn't want more than a hundred square feet, which made me more of a nuisance than a customer, and that I would like to have it in a week or so as my program was geared to cucumbers. He said, "Cucumbers? Oh, no, no—not at all! We've got to start somewhere, ha-ha!" He, however, had not seen any Transpeek, but hoped the factory would deliver soon. He hoped I wouldn't have to wait too long. I told him that here in Maine we didn't have much to do all winter but wait, and he promised to be back soon.

Now comes Corporation D, just named wholesale outlet for New England. The man told me over the telephone that since retail outlets had not been set up, he would accord me wholesale privileges for the time being, and would ship me whatever quantity I wanted at C.O.D. I said this was no good, since I had long ago told the post office and all other carriers and forwarders that I refuse all C.O.D. parcels. So he said, "Then I suggest you establish credit and we'll carry you on open account."

This brings us to Corporations E, F, and G, which are bilateral participants and figure only as credit references. I seem to remember they were General Motors, U.S. Steel, and the Pennsylvania Railroad. All I know about credit is that I pay my bills promptly, and these references seemed good—in a few days I received a roll of Transpeek and it seemed to be just what I wanted. The whole roll weighed far less than glass, and the strength seemed right. It was fun to realize I was pioneering Transpeek and would have the only plastic cucumber frames in the whole State of Maine!

We now return to Corporation A, to which I expressed thanks, adding that Transpeek seemed like a fine product, and asking what I should use for an adhesive to bond Transpeek to wood. Their reply was immediate. No experiments had been made as to an adhesive. They just made Transpeek; they didn't stick it. However, their chemists suggested butyl acetate, ethyl acetate, styrene, and any similar product which would be available at any store which carries them. Or, I could apply to Corporations H, I, J, K, L, and M. I didn't try all of them, but I did write to Corporation K. Corporation K thanked me for writing. They said they made a product that competed with Transpeek, and an adhesive for it, but they didn't know if their adhesive would work on Transpeek. They felt methyl methacrylate polymer would work, but they didn't make that. I could get some from Corporation N, whose address was enclosed. Or, if I wanted to try methyl dicrocuspid polyplatus cresylite, I should "contact" Corporation O, adhesives division.

Winter was breaking up now. For somebody who just wanted a dozen cucumber frames I had been well entertained. I wrote to Corporation O, and they sent me three small sample tubes which I could try. Meantime, their salesman would call on his next trip and I could order in quantity.

The lumber for my cucumber frames cost, at that time, less than five dollars, and the roll of Transpeek was six plus express charges. I used only part of the roll on my frames. I never did buy any adhesive. The stuff Corporation O sent me in the tubes proved to be solvents for Transpeek, and also ate off the bristles of the brush I used to apply them. Instead of an adhesive, I just painted the frames with green paint, and while the paint was still wet I laid in the Transpeek and the drying paint made it adhere. I had the paint in an old can, so it was very cheap. My frames lasted for years. Postage, tolls, and time, all those corporations must have spent a good ten thousand dollars to bother with me. And I don't know an acetate from an ethyl, but I'm a leading authority on American Industry.

Except Loose Teeth

When our summer people go home at Labor Day because the schools are about to open, our schools are about to open, too, and at least once before they close again next spring

I like to go and visit. We taxpayers are everywhere urged to take an interest in the schools and keep an eye on how things are going, but not many of us do. We should. This time, when I showed up unannounced and introduced myself and my purpose, the teacher wrung my hand warmly and said he was sorry I had picked this particular day—it was assembly day and that was all right, but the men had come to fix the roof. Every time something good happened, according to him, somebody came to fix something. He said I had no idea what teachers have to put up with.

This is probably important. For long years now I have been assaulted with propaganda from the school people meant to entice me towards bigger appropriations, and a good part of the argument has always been that I have no idea what teachers put up with. I've been told about the long years they put in at school and college at great expense, burning the midnight oil to acquire a license to be underpaid. We hear that school buildings are outmoded, that facilities are too small, and all such as that. Best argument of all has always been that we mustn't deprive our poor, dear chee-ildren of their educations by being parsimonious about finger painting and volleyball. Truth to tell, none of these excellent arguments has impressed me too much. I don't think somebody learning to be a teacher burnt any more midnight oil than I did or applied himself with more zeal. Teachers enjoy the security of the public payroll, which I never did and never will, and from my frugal comfort I fancy most teachers earn more money than I do. There may have been a year or two that I was rich in things like salted-down cucumbers, and there have been winters saddened by too many vinegar pies. I picked my way and the schoolmarm picked hers, and no skin off our noses, but I've never cried poor mouth as some schoolmarms do. Which isn't saying much, because if somebody brings me a basket of watermelons, I'll take it. On the other hand, to think thus is to think constructively, and I wouldn't want to be a schoolmarm. I wouldn't like it, and nobody comes around to beseech me to be kind to schools and schoolmarms for reasons

I will buy. Well, no superintendent of schools ever got up in a town meeting to beg higher taxes and asked us citizens how we'd like to sit in front of a class of thirty youngsters who are all wiggling their loose front teeth. I respond lackadaisically to the anguished appeal for bigger and better field hockey showers, but I'll gladly contribute to teachers who watch the loose teeth so I don't have to.

I believe all teachers who teach the loose-tooth grades are underpaid. They ought to get four and five times as much, fringes to their hips, and every other day off. But we hear about cost-of-living increases, summer-school expenses, long extra hours correcting papers, and everything else except loose teeth.

It was disconcerting that day I visited school to have the work-men on the roof. The bell summoned the scholars to assembly so they could demonstrate their learning to a visiting taxpayer, and at the same time the men put up a ladder past the school-room windows. The men were making joshing banter that couldn't be ignored, and the teacher had a little trouble gaining order. After some opening remarks, the program began with a violin solo by a young lady with braces and yellow curls, and she fingered moderately as if her father had told her not to wear out the strings. Her first few notes suggested Mendelssohn's *Spring Song*, but the music was overplayed by a man on the roof who shouted, "Hey, Charlie—push it this way a foot!" The little girl did play on, suggesting that intrusions from the uncultured outside world were not uncommon in the halls of learning, and the men pounded on the roof with hammers. "Contrapuntal," I murmured gently to myself.

Next was a boy with a recitation. He lowered his chin on his chest, took a deep breath, and began. But the words I heard were, "Joe, bring up the tallygloop!"

"What say, Hank?"

"I say, bring up a polterstarn!"

"They's one up there!"

"I need a big one!"

"Okay."

"Never mind—I got one!"

The teacher looked drawn and tired. He had gone to college and earned his lot by degrees. He had dedicated himself to his career. He was up every morning before breakfast, and in the evening after the PTA meeting he would correct papers and prepare the morrow's program. Nobody had told him that he would work for an idiot superintendent who always had the men come to fix the roof on assembly days. And nobody tells this to us taxpayers.

After school, I lingered to quiet the poor man down and express my concern, and he said fixing the roof is nothing compared to having the furnace cleaned on music day. He says the furnace men work in the pickle shops and the shoe factories all the rest of the time, but on music days they come and pound on the basement pipes. Then he told me about the time he had the movie about the cocoa industry. This is a popular educational movie, much in demand, and schools have to wait their turn. He had been waiting almost the whole school year for it, and the day he got it was the day the electricians came to rewire the exercising machines in the teachers' lounge. They pulled the main switch, and he had no juice for his projector.

I asked him why he didn't write an article about things like that and put it in the town report so we taxpayers would know what a teacher has to put up with. He said he'd think about it, but right now he couldn't get to do any work at his desk until the plasterers were finished.

With Four Humps

T elevision does embellish many a dreary Maine winter evening, but not always the way the television people think. It's when television puts us in mind of something else and we withdraw to think things over and meditate. Well, I was just watching a well-recommended show on the public, or dunning, channel that was supposed to be about life back on the old farm, and in comes a fellow with a bucket and he humps on a barnyard pump exactly four times and goes away with a pail of water that is running over and splashing all around the place. He was going to water a horse. I had the cat on my knee and a pan of popcorn akimbo, and I thought I was going to be edified until bedtime. Instead, I shut off the set and considered the truth about old-time pumps. That one on the television was probably made of Styrofoam and painted rusty and connected to a city water system. I suppose a highly paid technician turned a backstage valve while the boy with the bucket pumped four times. Until we got electricity on the farm and piped the hillside bubbling spring into the house and barn, we lived with pumps, and I know you don't get a pail of water with four humps.

And I'm not going back all that far. The chain pump in our barnyard was old, but it still worked in its desultory way. The endless chain went down into the well and up again as the crank was turned, and little cups brought water up through a pipe to spill it into the cattle's drinking tub. When new, a chain pump was a marvel, but after a few weeks it lost its precision, and most of the water would drip back past the cups and never get to the top. An uncle, who cranked that same chain pump as a boy, developed a spiritual philosophy from it. He used to tell how he would come home from school on a brisk January afternoon and approach his chore as custodian of the chain pump. He would stand there in the windswept barnyard cranking the thing to bring up water for forty-seven cows, sixteen young stock, four horses, ten sheep, and a bull—plus several pailsful for slopping the pigs. He told me this led him to run away from home when he was twelve, and enlightened him about the hereafter. Uncle said that a boy who knew about chain pumps in a January barnyard would never fear the perpetual fires of Hell. Uncle always assured me he looked forward to the promise of everlasting heat.

The piston pump we had on our kitchen sink shelf was a vast improvement over a chain pump. Using atmospheric pressure, in theory it would lift water thirty-two feet, but the manufacturer acknowledged certain coefficients of loss, and hedged at about twenty-two. Our house well then was maybe twenty feet deep and never had more than three feet of water in it, and our house sat up on a knoll with the sink shelf thirty-two inches above the kitchen floor, so we weren't supposed to be able to get any water at all. But after priming the pump we could get a pail of water with just about a hundred strokes.

We never had a freeze-up with the chain pump—water leaked back into the well by itself before ice could form, even in far-minus weather. But the pump on the sink shelf had notches cut into the suction leather so it would drain itself—and if you think kitchens were warm enough in those times to keep a pump from freezing you ought to be running a television show yourself. When a kitchen pump started to "run down" after somebody used it, there was dramatic entertainment for the whole family.

The family would be around the kitchen table with its kerosene lamp. A folksy tableau—verisimilitude in the old family kitchen. Somebody would go to the sink and pump for about ten minutes and get himself a glass of water. (Not a glass, really—there was a family tin dipper known as a "bumper.") Now the pump would begin to run down, to drain itself before it froze. The first note in the drain-out rendition was a long gasp, like huh-h-h-h-h-hrh-rh-uh-uh-uh. This was when enough water had seeped through the notches to create a vacuum in the barrel of the pump, causing the plunger to descend and the handle to erect. From position six-o'clock, the handle would rise to high twelve, keeping time with the syllables of the long gasp. Since there was no foot valve on the pipeline to the well, everything was now downhill, and the family would sit there and listen to a succession of rumbles, bumbles, gurgles, wheezes, glups and blups, and numerous frequent whistles. In time all the water in the pump and pipe would have drained back into the well, and with a final triumphant whooooomph the pump would return to silence. You might say the show was over, but during all this drain-out we—the family—didn't pay any attention. The pump handle, the vacuum gone, would now descend silently to position six-o'clock, and all was ready for the next bumper of water.

Priming the pump gave us another concert. Vigorously working the handle, the pumpist would pour a cupful of priming water in at the top of the pump, and then, stroke by stroke, would exhaust the air in the pump and pipe, and gradually bring well water to the top. The ascending water kept shortening the column of air in the pipe, so the effect was exactly that of a pipe organ, the stops running about six octaves. Then somebody would say, "There she comes!" and with a refreshing gurgle water would appear at the spout.

But there was no such thing as a pailful of water in four humps of the handle. That had to wait for television.

With Gumption

I n the winter, the Maine roads less traveled by run to the north. We like to head in that direction along in the drear December, and even in the frosty Feb., and truthfully, we have found more fun that-a-way than we have in t'other. And, we like back roads. The turnpikes don't have mailboxes and kitchen windows alight and front dooryards. Nobody lives on throughways. It's far better to roam the byways and climb the hills and keep in touch with people. So we were on our way home now from a few days in Quebec Province, just to break up our winter routine, and we'd be home in a couple of hours.

So she said, "Better find a place to pick up a loaf of bread."

She had been taking feminine inventory. As we rode along I was admiring woodpiles and wondering how many cows to a barn, and she had been checking out the shelves and cupboards back home. What did we need for provisions? Bread—yes. Bread we'd need until she could bake some.

Before long we came to a fork in the road and there was a store. I pulled up.

"And I guess some prunes," she added.

This was far from somewhere. It was a cold day. It was back in the woods, you might say, except that today you can have about anything back in the woods. I expected the store to have what I wanted. You see frozen food cases about everywhere. But when I pulled open the door and stepped in, there was a difference. The store had a wood fire in a wood-burning stove.

It smelled good. It's hard to burn wood without releasing a spurt of woodsmoke every time you add a stick, but in addition to that a wood fire gives off its own special kind of heat that no other fuel can match. A wood fire, with a touch of smoke in the air, does smell good, but it also *feels* good. It's a thing to back up to, and in a country store with a wood stove the customer should always absorb a little comfort before opening negotiations. The store was warm when I stepped in, and it grew warmer as I went forward towards the stove. I went past a stand of axes and a couple of chain saws on the floor, and past a display of felt boots. Real down-Maine larrigans. This was lumber and pulpwood country and winter goods had prominence. Then there was a fellow sitting by the stove—just sitting—and he was gray and elderly. Mackinaw and mittens on, cap down over his ears, he didn't look up at me. He hadn't known I was due to come in, so he hadn't made arrangements to look up. A man the whole town probably called Gramp. Now a young woman came from a back room.

"Hi!" she said.

I said, "Hi!"

I also said, "Fire sure feels some good!"

She said, "Be colder weather 'fore it gets warmer."

I said, "Oh, stay cheerful—it's bound to warm up before June."

"One summer we had winter right into August," said the old man.

I've reported this carefully, because I believe there are expatriate people present who don't know how conversation should run in a Maine back-country store in the cold season. They may not believe we still have stores with axes on display and an old man at the stove—a stove, even—and a store where talk is just as important as the final twang of the cash register.

"Can't beat a wood fire," I said.

"Best kind," she said.

"None better," said the old man.

The woman said, "Stays cold so I have to get up middle the night and put in wood. Freeze things up if I di'n't. Gen'ally this stove holds a fire till morning, hot ashes, anyway—but with this cold snap I got to leave the damp-puh a mite free."

"Can't you get oil here?" I asked, but only to hear what she'd say.

"Oh, sure. But I'd look sweet buying oil on the profits of what gross-rees I sell here. I got ten men cutting hardwood, and if I just took one stick out of every cord I couldn't burn that much."

She opened the stove, poked the fire, and shoved in another stick. "Not that I do," she added. "But I could—the scalers would never know."

"Big selling point for oil," I offered, "was always the ease and comfort—no ashes to lug out, automatic—like that."

"That's all yes and no. Oil is fine, but Old John D.'s got all he needs without help from me. I got fifteen hundred acres on Gifford Mountain I pay taxes on, and wood just lays around. I can keep that stove red hot and it don't cost me a cent."

The store door opened and closed, and it was my goodwife coming in to find out what had happened to me. "Oh, smell the wood fire," she says. Then she says, "I burn wood at home."

"Best to bake by, on top of the heat," said the old man.

"I want some baking powder, too," she said to me.

"Baking pow-duh," said the woman. "Anything else?"

"Bread and prunes," I said.

"I got loose ones and tight ones."

"Loose ones is best," said the old man. "Cook up better and show more gumption."

"Loose prunes it is," I said.

"Best kind," said the old man.

So we paid and we drove along, after the woman had asked us to stop in again. The bread had lingered about two days too many, but the prunes were magnificent. We cooked them on a wood fire and they mulled with gumption. So we came home from our little winter trip, glad for a country store that is hotter than a two-dollar pistol in a cold January, kept so by preference and prudence in the day of supers. It's on a road less traveled by, right at the fork, back a piece.

The First Word

There was a time my protracted hibernation was pleasantly interrupted by the annual spelling bee. I believe in spelling bees more than I believe in the evaluated IQ, and much more than I do in the scholastic achievement tests, so I was happy to rise from my fireside armchair and brave the wintry blasts to go and be bee master and find out which of our dozen or so hopefuls would become county champion and go to the state finals. Perhaps even to the nationals. The customary routine was to assemble the contestants, each with a retinue of classmate rooters and a hopeful teacher, and then somebody would hand me the official word list for this year's bee. Nobody, even I, had seen this list before; it was drawn up by the national spelling bee committee and was being used simultaneously in every county contest countrywide. I naturally offered a few pleasantries and witticisms to set a mood, because I think spelling bees should be fun. When I thought the youngsters were at ease I'd begin with a few small words at the top of the list—cat, able, ease, dare, crowd, swamp, and such simplicities—and we'd have a couple of rounds with no casualties. Now and then we'd lose a contestant on the easy words, but not often, and we'd usually go a quarter of an hour with all the original contestants still standing. Then I'd skip to harder words, and find the old favorites like supersede and clarify, and the line would gradually thin down until we had a winner.

I said "there was a time," because I gave this up a few years back and don't do it any more. Something happened to the Big Shot committee that runs this national scholastic sport, and I guess the members began thinking like the Miss America people and the Rose Bowl crowd. I came that year as usual, and as usual we had the bright-looking bunch of hopefuls. The teachers and the rooters sat in order, and I began warming up with my comical remarks. And I said, "All right, enough of this persiflage—p-e-r-s-i-f-l-a-g-e—let's find out which of you is going to the state contest!"

Then I looked at the list of words supplied by the national committee, and the first word was bacillus.

"Bacillus," I said.

The youngsters all looked blank. They shifted to look at each other, and then turned to look at their teachers. Then they turned to look at me. "Bacillus," I repeated. It was the first word on the list.

The sweet young miss at the head of the line, a green ribbon on her carrot hair, took a deep breath and said, "Would you please use that in a sentence, please?"

This is proper, but not usually asked about the very first word on the list. And I found myself standing there without the faintest idea of how to use bacillus in a sentence. Things did mesh shortly, but it was disconcerting to think this contretemps came from one little bacillus, too small to see with the naked eye. Then I fell to wondering if they use Latin plurals these days, or should I say bacilluses. By this time everybody except the bee master was convinced the bee master was giving out words he didn't even know himself. So I, now, took a deep breath and I told the lovely little redhead that a bacillus is a bacterium, of which the plurals are, or ought to be, bacilli and bacteria, any of various microscopic vegetable organisms.

She said, "What?"

That year our contest didn't last long. The idiots who made up the word list misjudged the grammar-school potential. I handed out words like bibliophile, consanguinity, daguerreotype, and eleemosynary with the carnage of the Roman legions racing through Gaul as a whole, and one by one my little friends sat down. One word was foraminifera, which I'd never seen before and didn't know how to pronounce, and I hope I never see it again. The whole bee ran about three minutes.

I was immediately attacked en masse by the teachers, who cried foul. They said they wanted to enter a formal protest. I tried to explain that I was no more than an innocent bystander, that I had been done in by the same idiots who made up the list of words. All I do, I kept saying, is read off what they give me. One teacher said, "I'm so surprised—always before you've been so fair and honest!"

Thus I learned that no spelling match should ever use words the scholars can't spell. Words such as I had been given could cause serious intellectual trauma to an innocent child. The contestant has the right to assume that any word submitted will offer a reasonable chance to exhibit prowess. The kid has his rights; I had done an underhanded thing. A bee master has a responsibility to be fair, they said. So I could see that under the teachers' code none of their tots would ever get spelled down, something I'm sure none of them would argue except that the suddenness of this year's demise had beguiled them. One teacher said, "Why, what you have done to these poor little children is a terrible thing."

As I rode home, I realized the only thing I had proved is that nobody in our county can spell monocotyledon. I had to admit I couldn't, anyway. I tried to rationalize that if tentaculocyst is on the list, first or last, somebody is going to get it one round or another, but such logic crumbles before the fact that for the first time our county spelling bee hadn't been any fun for anybody. I sent along my regrets that henceforth on the day of the annual spelling bee I would have a prior engagement.

The Only One

There's not much call for a necktie in the summer, but after the fall and winter social season sets in I get mine out and use it now and then. I was accordingly interested to see in the Christmas advertising that a maker of neckties now puts on a little tag that tells you the color scheme. You can turn one of his ties over and the tag says, "Wear with brown suit." My philosophy about neckties has been influenced by several things, and one is a thirteen-volume cyclopedia published by Carey & Lee in Philadelphia of 1830. The thing is fun to read because the information is so outdated and useless. Under "cravat" this cyclopedia voices my sentiments:

> CRAVAT—An unhealthy, uncomfortable, unbecoming article of European and American dress. The ancients were unacquainted with this ridiculous and injurious style of bundling up the neck . . .

In spite of my agreement with that, I do have a necktie. When I put it on, which is as seldom as I can manage, I wear it with my suit. If the color scheme is socially askew, I'm sorry. If I should turn my necktie over and it tells me to wear with a brown suit—my suit is charcoal gray.

When I see today's happy and muscle-bound children waiting for the school bus in casual attire that would not have been approved in my time, their total garb relaxed and indifferent, I can see that the necktie has fallen from fashion. In my time, all boys wore neckties. If for any reason I didn't put my tie on before starting the long walk to school, the girls would mock me and point at me and sing-song, "Johnnie forgot his necktie!"

I used to wear detachable collars. With a clean collar every morning, I could get three days out of a shirt, and before mechanical home laundries that was a fine thing. And if I forgot my necktie, there would be a big brass collar button sticking out in front, shining in the morning light. The forgotten necktie would have covered that button and left me less conspicuous. The girls thought a naked collar button was comical. There was a second collar button at the back of the neck that went with those detach-able collars, but it didn't show up because it was hidden by the collar of the proper jacket that every boy then wore. The turtle-neck and the sport shirt had not been thought up, then, and a shirt collar open at the neck was rude. That front collar button was mooring for a trick necktie I owned for a time. This necktie was already tied, permanently, when I got it as a Christmas present, and it didn't have any part that went around behind my neck. Instead, it had a wire loop that fastened onto that front collar button. It was really a great idea—I could grab the tie and hang it on and scoot for school. The tie went on that easy, and it looked like a good four-in-hand, but it also had an easiness about popping off. I never knew when it had jumped its tether, but I never lost it because it was the only one of its kind in school. Somebody would bring it to me and I'd hang it back on the collar button. One of the girls used to say she'd found it in the girls' basement, but she just made that up to be funny.

Odd, in a way, that I had that necktie I didn't have to tie, because I was a good necktie tier. I could do it without looking in a mirror, holding my head up to keep my chin out of the way. We had a neighbor, Mr. Moulton, who used to come into our kitchen in the morning just to watch me do it. He was never able to tie his own tie and always had to have his wife do it, so he thought I was pretty nifty. But I never owned so many ties that I was perplexed about which color to wear. I kept a subdued pattern for Sundays, and then I had my other one for school. The school tie would achieve a sheen and a patina and developed a disciplined reflex so it looked tied when it was on the back of a chair. Once in a while it would get washed. I don't remember that I ever bought a necktie—somebody in the family would notice that I was wearing a disreputable tie to school and on my next birthday, or for Christmas, my present would be a new necktie. One time I made a necktie. There was a small joke we'd hear now and then when somebody appeared with a necktie of questionable taste. "Do you make your own neckties?" he would be asked. So just for fun I saved the cotton threads that we pulled out of grain bags, and I knitted me a necktie. Mother stuck it in a dye-pot with some rug rags and it came out a funereal purple that caught all eyes. Then, when people asked if I made my own neckties I said that I did. It's the only one I ever made, and if it hadn't been in jest it was the kind of necktie nobody would wear to a dogfight. But I did wear a tie—all boys wore ties. We lived in an orderly society that did things right; nobody of consequence would materially err. We were intended to be little gentlemen, and a necktie was proof of gentility.

I stand on that. I still keep my necktie handy in the bureau drawer, so I can reach it speedily at the first threat of gentility. In a social context, I am prepared. But this new bit about which color I wear with which suit has me baffled. The only tag on my necktie says, "Dry clean only."

Waiting to Hear

A determined program of hot mince pie will allay the doldrums of a down-Maine cold spell, so I took a reaction to the news from Iowa—I probably pronounce that wrong—that they have mincemeat now with no meat in it. Some food processor out there is offering mincemeat without meat in it, and tests and trials have given it a good rating. Some busybody purists have lifted a semantic lament that it shouldn't be called mincemeat if it lacks meat, so in this kind of a give-and-take it is entirely possibly the entire state of Iowa is waiting to hear from me.

This whole thing is part of the new-day gradual departure from the basic theory that food should be nourishing. It was a big shock to me when I first heard of a meatless meat pie. Then I met the skinless frankfurter. I asked the waitress how they held a skinless frankfurter together, and she said there was nothing in the things anyway so it didn't matter. Next I met the meatless meat loaf. This one belongs to the respectable, if peculiar, self-discipline of the vegetarians, and in that context we have to accept it. If you like hamburgers made from soybeans and skimmed milk, you are protected by the Constitution, and it is my duty to defend to starvation your right to do so, but it seems to me mincemeat without meat in it has drawn the issue out into a major threat.

Here in Maine we draw from pioneer beginnings to maintain that pies are to cut wood on. That is, you tuck away a piece of pie and it will sustain you at your work, whereas food that digests on you is a sham and imposter. A pie was meant to ingratiate itself into your substance, to linger and contribute. Any truly good dessert will do as much—Indian meal pudding with happy lemon sauce, rice boiled with cinnamon and raisins. Useful as steam engines; good as a horse that trots all day. So, mince pie gave us Easterners the backbone and thrust to move forward and onward, the muscle to build things and build them well. Mince pie also gave the frugal housewife something to do with a venison neck. Mincemeat made with "deer meat" didn't need maple syrup and molasses and a rum sauce to make it "go some good," but those things added useful vigor. It could take a little butter, too. Full of the fortitude that comes with mince pie, the Easterners licked every problem, and some of them went to places like Iowa to do it.

Mince pie was never served cold, but was the forerunner of the frozen food business. The grandmothers made mince pies by the dozens in the fall of the year and froze them on a screened shelf in the shed. They'd bring one in as needed, heat it red hot in the oven, and warn everybody at table, "Mind, now—that pie's hot!" A tongue once scalded by hot mince pie will never forget it. We had an uncle who told about the time he was an unexpected guest at dinner. The hostess hadn't expected him, so hadn't "het" the pie. So she brought one frozen from the shed without time to thaw it. (Uncle always said *unthaw* it.) Uncle got a piece that was still stiff and cold, and he said, "I et it, just to spite her."

Iowans will need to know that store-bought mincemeat is hardly a new product; Maine food suppliers have offered it for generations. It comes a little bland, and always the same—the homemade kind offers a variable rule-of-thumb by which every loving mother makes mincemeat her own way. Besides, canning factory mincemeat lacks a certain something—see recipe below. And, you don't get venison neck in the store-bought kind—good cull beef, maybe, but not the real stuff. Even so, it is honest—it doesn't belong to the new belief that good food makes you skinny. So perhaps we should not be unkind to the food processors who offer us mincemeat without meat. Wouldn't it be smarter to worry about the American consumer who is willing to spend his good money for something that isn't there?

Mincemeat should have, for a decent family orgy, four pounds of lean meat in it. Beef if you have no deer meat. Then you want two pounds of beef suet. Grind the meat and the suet with the coarse wheel of your grinder—don't try to chop-chop as some idiot cookbooks say. Now look at the amount of meat and suet you have, and grind up enough apples to double the quantity. Three pounds of sugar, two cups of molasses, three quarts of cider, three pounds of raisins, three pounds of currants, a half pound of candied citron. Then, one-half tablespoon of cinnamon, one-half tablespoon of mace, one tablespoon of cloves, and two grated nutmegs. A teaspoon of black pepper, and "just enough" salt.

It's a good idea to cook your meat and suet a day ahead, covering the blend in a pot with boiling water and taking it off when tender. Do NOT throw away the water! Now, you can mix the cooked meat with the other things—but not the spices yet—and things are looking good. In the pot that cooked the meat you have the water. Boil it down until it amounts to a cup and a half, and add it to the mixture. Now you heat the mixture gradually, stirring it always clockwise so it doesn't unwind, and it should have a couple of hours, at least, of moderate heat, with an occasional stir. Two hours more or less, and then add the spices. Stir and simmer, and shortly all is ready to be bottled. But before the jars (Mason jars are just fine) are covered, you want to do what the commercial food processors do not do in the canning factories—you want to add a decent dollop of brandy or rum to each jar. This will show everybody that you have a generous disposition. It will also season your mincemeat so nobody at your table is ever going to ask what store it came from. However, as with all reputable and reliable State-o'-Maine recipes, make allowances. A recipe to a Maine mother is something to go by, not something to follow. In every

Maine recipe there is the priceless and unmeasured ingredient of a loving hand, usually with a worn wedding ring, and there is no cookbook extant that can help you with that. So now your mincemeat is safe on the shelf to ripen and make glad the people. Somebody from Iowa might stop by, and you can bring him the Truth and the Light.

Approved List

A good town library with a comely librarian is an excellent influence for joy during the January retirement, and we have both a good town library and a comely librarian. Nancy looks up when the door opens and calls her happy hello to neighbors and townsfolk on a first-name rating, and an intense literary fellowship accrues which defeats the most sullen thermometer. I do wonder what joys are found in tropical shuffleboard every time I step from a cold blast into Nancy's presence and come away not only in renewed spirits but with a couple of good books.

When I was in school we never had a school library as such. Andrew Carnegie had given us a building, and the town had made annual appropriations to fill it with proper books. Whenever any schoolwork called for research in the golden realms we'd go to the town library. The school did have a short shelf that was meant for dictionaries—Webster, German-English, French-English, Latin-English. That was our school library, except for five volumes of a seventy-five-year-old encyclopedia that had everything in it except what anybody wanted to know. The teachers told us not to bother with it, but to go to the town library. It was on the occasion of my twentieth class reunion from high school that the hat was passed to help raise money so our school might at last have its own library.

And back when I was twenty years "out," a ten dollar bill would buy at least two books in a bookstore, and three with the librarian's discount. So my class added a couple of hundred to the fund and later that year we each got a letter of thanks from the principal, with a list of the books he had bought with our generous gift. It was interesting that he had spent seventy-five dollars more than we had donated, and he explained how this could be. Some of the books he had bought were on the "approved list" of the National Defense Administration, so there would be a reimbursement from the federal government on those titles just as soon as his purchase could be "finalized." Those were, indeed, the glad days of enthusiastic federal aid in all directions, and we humble citizens had been assured all along that there would be no "federal control" to go along with federal aid. Possibly somebody believed that. So here was the tip-off as to how federal control managed its affairs. These titles that were to be "approved" in Washington were all technical, hefty on the side of physics and leaning towards the nuclear future. Let us observe it was not the policy of the National Defense Administration to subsidize *Alice's Adventures in Wonderland*. "I guess you don't need to learn everything in school," I said to myself. Yes, I did.

The first librarian in my life was Miss Annette Aldrich. A spare and untarnished spinster from a long time of seafaring ancestors, she could afford to be librarian in our town because there was "family income." The job didn't pay much, and the janitor who attended the coal furnace, swept up, and emptied the trash got more than Miss Aldrich. And, fear not, she was *always* called *Miss* Aldrich; none of this foolish Ms. stuff. She was maybe seventy-five, going on eighty. Miss Aldrich presided, and that is exactly the word for it. She never greeted anybody with the becoming affability of my Nancy of later life, but might extend a modest recognition with a slight nod. She wore lace choke-collars and had a bosom gold watch on a chain, with a fleur-de-lis. Dignity was her word. Her desk had regal quality, and she reigned. But she was a bundle of noblesse oblige and whenever I presented her a problem she turned all out to find what I needed. My recollection assures me she contributed far more to some of my school grades than any teacher ever did. And when she was satisfied she had found me the proper books to further my knowledge and understanding, she would hand me something like *Joe Strong the Boy Fish* and ask if I'd read that one. One day she handed me *Pudd'nhead Wilson*, no doubt surmising it would make me a good place to start.

Miss Aldrich's burden was lack of funds. The small appropriation approved at annual town meeting covered not only her salary, but that of the janitor, heat and light, and the rebinding of veteran books. Besides lack of money, she was restricted, or guided, by our library trustees, who were respectable and trustworthy men who could be counted on to authorize only respectable and trustworthy books. There was never a question in my time about naughty books on our library shelves. Twice a year a box of new books would arrive from a wholesaler. After Miss Aldrich cataloged the books they would go on a shelf marked NEW BOOKS and would have that distinction until the next box of new books came. Otherwise, Miss Aldrich had the old books, and some of them were very.

The serenity of our little library would be shattered whenever Miss Aldrich let go with one of her horrendous sneezes. When I would come and approach her at her desk and inquire about such-and-such, she would lay her lead pencil (it had a rubber stamp attached with the date a book must be returned) alongside her nose, look studiously aloft, say hm-m-m-m-m, and rise from her throne with an "I think maybe . . ." Then I would follow her behind the shelves until she would pick down a book and look at the title. She'd nod at it. Then she would do the most wonderful thing—a gesture that has come to mean, to me, the whole essence and being of a library. She would open the book at its middle, hold it at arms' length, and then slap it shut again with a resounding bang that would make all

the magazine readers at the tables look up. It was a bang that, unless the librarian made it, would never be tolerated in a library. This clap would burst forth a great cloud of erudite and sapient dust, the accumulation of long literary desuetude, and it would billow and bulge along the aisle. Then, because she was allergic to dust, Miss Aldrich would sneeze. Not a simple, small, decorous, ladylike sneeze suited to the gentility of Miss Aldrich, who was forever a lady, but one that rattled the framed picture of Mr. Carnegie on the wall and shook Miss Aldrich away back into her maritime ancestry. It wracked her from stem to stern. She held nothing back; she gave it her all. From this sneeze Miss Aldrich would recover with a shake of her shoulders, and she would return to her desk and stamp the due date in the book so I could go home and do my schoolwork.

So, when I peeled off a bill at that twentieth class reunion and felt generous about supporting a new school library, I had Miss Aldrich in mind, and I was really making a small donation in her memory. I certainly was not thinking about a year's subscription to a hot rod magazine, *Earth Science, Elements of the Universe,* and other diesel-fired and nuclear-based reading matter that has the approval of the National Defense Administration and pays government refunds. I guess I was thinking about Poe and Hawthorne, and Mark Twain, and Dickens and Cooper and Irving, and how a sneeze from Miss Aldrich was an experience in culture.

Half the Price

My winter thoughts are comfortably beguiled by the advertising that starts, "According to a national survey . . ." Since I was never surveyed in a national survey, I feel entitled to my doubts that any national survey was ever made. But let us suppose, for the sake of amusement, that this advertising is truthful and as the result of a national survey nine out of ten Americans prefer the mild laxative. How would you like to be a surveyist who goes from one end of the country to the other asking people about their bowels? I wouldn't, and I don't believe any national survey was ever made that supports the milder laxative; I think the advertising lies. So, as I put in my time with seasonal rumination, it occurs to me that what this great nation needs is a fancy and well-heeled foundation that will fund authentic, objective, unbiased surveys and reports that will counteract authentic, objective, unbiased reports now being done by foundations that have a lot of money.

These surveys that need counteraction are excellent surveys, done with the highest quality of academic accuracy, with great protestation of equanimity, and served to us in the finest oblique language which is its own proof of unimpeachable authority. I like the way the survey people have adopted ambiguity; if the

public can't understand, the public will buy. Validity of weasel-worded surveys is certified (1) by the great expense incurred, and (2) by the eminence of the surveyist, who will be at least a professor. Most of the surveys I have ever known about could just as well have been done by me at half the price, even two for the cost of one, but I am not a professor. The unbiased nature of my bias is not academically rooted.

Of course I'm bitter about this. We have amongst us all manner of honest, sincere, intelligent, and informed people who can never become "experts" because they lack college degrees. Some of our biggest boobs adorn college faculties, and because they hide behind their doctorates we confuse them with scholars. Some poor slob who never finished high school but owns half the hotels in Miami will never be asked to do a survey on hotel management—that survey will be done by some simpleton who fanatically sleeps in elder-hostels and has more degrees than a Masonic thermometer. So I think I shall enunciate a parable:

Along about the time of the Great World War to make things safe for democracy, the Maine clam fell upon evil days. The Maine clam is the long-neck, softshell kind, and is not to be mistaken for the quahog, which is esteemed elsewhere but not much in Maine. For a long time the Maine clam had been a big money-maker for coastal people, and the finest kind of prosperity was to own a few acres alongshore with a path between the potato patch and the clam flat. That is, life was good with a neat house by a garden and access to the tide. But civilization, so-called, was taking its toll of the poor clam. Forests had been logged off, which lifted river temperatures and changed the ocean enough to make a difference. Eelgrass began to move in, and eelgrass kills clams. People, in growing numbers, had their effect. Clams began to be in short supply where once they throve, and it was clearly time to do something.

The difficulty was that nobody knew much about clams. The clam sits there in the mud under water, available to man only on the brief ebb tide, and there had been no effort to study him on his level and become acquainted with his way of life. This was back before the days of our modern surveys, but without knowing about surveys as such, somebody decided a survey of the clam was needed so that legislation could be prepared and enacted. Well, there was this fellow from 'way down east who got himself elected to the Maine legislature, and when he put in a bill to do something about the clam he wrote out a little report that was meant to support his arguments. Understand, at that time nobody knew anything about the gentle art of fabricating reliable information and correlating accurate statistics. But this fellow set down everything he knew about the clam, speaking not as an academic expert, but as one who had dug clams. True, he knew as much about clams as anybody, but he wasn't trying to produce what we would now consider a survey. His paper wasn't much, but at the time it was everything. It gained the validity that comes from "if you see it in print, it's so."

Sophisticated copying machines weren't ready yet, so this legislator had some copies of his paper run off on a mimeograph machine. Fellow members of the legislature all got copies, and this was enough to get the first clam bill passed. Then, a copy was lodged in the archives of the Maine State Library, where it reposes today among the legislative documents of our glorious past.

Meantime, the "survey" was invented and burst into fragrant bloom, and became a big thing in American life. All at once unbiased studies flourished, grants were forthcoming, and doctors of philosophy reveled in a new prosperity. The grants came to be measured by their duration. A professor would be given a grant to do an unbiased study and produce an unbiased survey, and he never asked what he was supposed to look into— he would ask how long the grant would run. A grant for a year was good, but a grant for only two months was something else again. And it was bound to happen—as subjects for academic surveys became harder and harder to trump up, somebody gladly thought of clams.

There's a smile to the very idea. How do you study a meditating clam, his hands folded in penitent posture, everything about him tight inside his shell and no way to reach him without disturbing the accumulated serenity of millennia? But a substantial grant from any reliable foundation can wipe the smile away from the most frivolous countenance, and the Maine Department of Sea and Shore Fisheries sedately accepted funds to survey the clam. Over the next couple of decades or so the clam got surveyed whenever any money chanced along, and on each occasion the Commissioner of Sea and Shore Fisheries would approve the report, acknowledge it with his initials, and hand a check to the grateful student who had just now become an expert on clams. In this way, over a few years, the structure and anatomy of the unbiased survey were put on record, and it was possible to go into the Maine State Library and do a dissection. Everything that everybody knew about the Maine clam started with the legislator from down east who mimeographed his report to support his bill. When a new professor got a new grant, he would go into the Maine State Library and take down everything there about the Maine clam. He would trace back through study after study and survey after survey, and at last he would come to that first mimeographed report. Having, now, everything at hand, he would rephrase it, regroup it, restate it, and reintroduce it in a manner that took him exactly three months, or whatever the term of the grant was. And you can go and look, and you'll find there isn't a thing in the latest unbiased survey and report that wasn't in the old duffer's mimeographed monograph in the beginning. True, "clams" have become "bivalve mollusks," and the price per peck is now pegged at "current economic impact." Scholarship has to keep up-to-date.

The impact of these many surveys of the clam varies according to what it was desired to prove at the time. That is, before undertaking an unbiased survey, the scholar has to find out which way he is expected to be unbiased. Objectivity must be kept headed in the right direction. Here, for instance, is a survey that starts, "It goes without saying that municipal managers have been successful." You know right away who's paying the bill—the National Association of Municipal Managers. What I propose is merely a countersurvey with equal lack of bias, which (were I to research it and write it) would start off, "These damned leeches . . ."

Thus the surveys interest me, and I don't begrudge a single minute I spend thinking about them.

A Working Anglican

Here in Maine the seasons vary with the Waltons and the Nimrods, and our gifted sports writers tell us that the Nimrods fare forth in the fall and the Waltons surge in the spring. This amounts to the changing of the guard when the law goes off. You don't fish when the law is "on"; you can go get your deer when the law is "off." There is something about this bandying of the names, and something about sports writers, that tells me Walton and Nimrod have been handed down from early sports writers who knew a few things to their successors, who don't always.

Nimrod is Biblical. He is in Genesis, in the generations of Noah, the son of Cush. It says he was a mighty hunter before the Lord; wherefore it is said, even as Nimrod, the mighty hunter before the Lord. He was the ruler of Sumeria and the builder of Nineveh—but only in the Book of Genesis; the Assyrian and Babylonian records don't mention him. When John Milton (who was not exactly a sports writer and could spell hard words) did his *Paradise Lost* he went to the Targum. The Targum is a body of translations, interpretations, and embellishments wherein briefer Biblical material is expanded. From the Targum John Milton gained a less vague picture of Nimrod, and found him a hunter of men, not beasts. Look in Book Twelve of the epic. Milton's Nimrod appears in that part of the story where prophecy is filling the gap between the world destroyed and the world restored—a less amusing part of the tale that most sports writers, busy with trapping muskrats and dressing deer, will have read fleetingly. Too bad, because the Maine deer hunt is never really doing well until the first Nimrod is arrested for "negligently shooting a relative out of season," an offense that carries a fine of $100.

But Isaac Walton is easier to get at, even if he does have some obscurities. In one book it says he was an ironmonger of Fleet Street, which could mean that he was a tin knocker amongst journalists, perhaps a sports writer. But another book says he was a linen draper of unspecified address, which sounds better. That his schooling was meager is agreed, but his writings show that he found some other way to improve his education. His *Compleat Angler* is not his only book, but his delightful biography of John Donne has brought him no particular esteem on the sports pages. Walton was a working Anglican as well as an artful angler, and he was a parishioner of Donne.

We, and all sports writers, should be more sensitive to this tidbit. To have listened to John Donne in the pulpit, or even to have passed his vicarage, is nothing to dismiss lightly. To have heard the voice of blind Homer; to have queried Socrates; to have seen even the dust of Shakespeare—to have sat in a pew while John Donne preached? Were you, kindest of friends, ever a small country boy whose good mother made him go to church on a fragrant apple-blossom Sunday in a Maine May, and you had to sit there and fidget a sermon while you thought about the trout leaping in Badger Brook? Then feel for Isaac Walton, the contemplative angler in John Donne's church.

Isaac Walton's prose has a melody that lingered from the Elizabethan period into the Restoration; a link betwixt. This makes *The Compleat Angler* important quite apart from the content, even if its content is still a great and distinct "only." It is the only how-to-do-it book to achieve high literary stature. It is a classic for its gentle philosophy, its tidy observations, its quiet prose in pleasing language. But it tells, merely, about fishing. How to select the bait, how to catch a fish, how to dress and cook one. No other author ever turned a more unlikely topic to a book of enduring charm. His biography of John Donne didn't, but his *The Compleat Angler* went through four editions in Walton's lifetime. Then his friend and brookside buddy, Charles Cotton, added some words about fly fishing that have become identified with the original work, and well over a hundred editions have appeared since Walton's death in 1683. Some of them are handsome gift volumes that angling-widows buy their husbands for Christmas. I got mine in 1938.

So I'm amused at going through Walton for a bid of midwinter promise of spring, smiling that so few Waltons do so. Oh, they know Nimrod was a hunter and Walton was a chaser of trout, but I've known 'em to guess Nimrod is from Scandinavian mythology and Walton was somebody like the Baron Munchausen describing a pickerel. I have, but not often, asked a sports writer if he's read Walton, and he didn't know he wrote anything. Too bad—a couple of casts over the Walton waters might improve the syntax of the sports pages.

The Distaff Reply

There has to be one good feed of new-run smelts while the snow water is running off and before May gets down to business, so I asked the boy down the road if he'd like to go with me and dip a few. He said no, because that was the night he went to get his marriage instructions—which is as bizarre a conflict of interest as I've met this winter. It certainly teased my reflective mind in all directions. In one direction, I wondered what they teach in these new-day seminars that instruct the rejoicing bridegroom, and then I pondered on what he truly needs to know. Such, for instance, as how to arrange to go smelting on that particular festive evening when the smelts first appear, whatever the alternative may be. But were I consulted about requisite understanding in order to be a successful husband, I would urge full instruction on the distaff reply.

Well, there was an afternoon I came into the house with pitch all over my hands after a bout with some green fir poles I was arranging into a grape arbor, and as I approached the sink to lave I beheld a bright, multicolored product of the demented weaver's highest art, a display equal to the massed banners at Agincourt, and something suitable for a snake charmer's tent at Topsham Fair. So, as a loving husband eager to take an interest in family affairs would, I asked, "What's that?" A straightforward, masculine, logical probe for information.

I make this clear, should any marriage instructors be listening—I was not trying to incubate a discussion or foment an argument. I had no intention of disturbing the peaceful atmosphere of our happy home. I merely wished to know what the thing was.

"Oh," she said, "I got that at the sale."

Smelting is a spring ritual which can also be considered an endurance contest, or a mortification of the flesh. It is more like torturous self-discipline than a clearly defined sport. A few reasons can be thought up to justify going for smelts, such as a feed of fried smelts, but it is much easier to think up reasons not to. But to the sensitive and inquisitive spirit, one which finds philosophic values where not always expected, going smelting offers a concomitant opportunity to think things over. So on that smelt expedition, alone in the dark by the swollen and ice-cold springtime brook, I kept thinking of the young man who was meantime being inculcated with prenuptial precepts, and I wondered if they were instructing him about the left-handed replies of brides of all ages.

The thing hanging by the sink—our sink, my sink—must have been something. It was clearly visible. It is well for the husband to take an interest—a good husband will never leave the door open for an "and you didn't even notice!" There has to be a sortie, and I had made one—now comes the intellectual challenge, the question of how many moves to win, as in checkers. To what ends must the loyal husband go to corner, rope, and tie the feminine answer? So I next said, which in retrospect seems to be a gentlemanly question and should have left me relatively secure, "Eyah, but what is it?"

She said, "It's from Stratford on Avon—it's got Shakespeare stuff on it."

So I was unable to get her to break away from the feminine rules that prevail in such sallies and to come right out and say, point-blank, "A dish towel." A dish towel which a husband should not expect to find emblazoned like an Alpine sunset and adorned with quotations from The Bard. A simple dish towel, meant for wiping dishes, and thus subject to reasonable inquiry when it looks like something an elephant wears in the Ringling spectacular. No simple man would ever presume a thing like that to be a dish towel—or a bedspread or an undershirt, or a strainer for new milk. I have no idea why dish towels come from Stratford on Avon, or why Shakespearean quotations should hang on a hook by the sink. And I never conferred with a marriage instructor, but I know very well that I mustn't ask.

The marriage seminars must, all the same, carefully teach that what is sauce for the goose is not sauce for the gander. I've tried it, and it won't work. There was the time I was rallying from a bout with the feminine reply, and I shoved my wallet in my pocket and pulled on my jacket, and she says, "Where are you off to?"

A proper question, pitched on reasonable curiosity. A clear, unmistakable inquiry. I hope the ladies will concede that her question is not all that different from mine. I asked about a dish towel; she asked about a destination. The upright, and safe, thing for me to say would be, "I'm going to the hardware store to get some hinges for the pump room window." A man's syllogisms are thus naturally arranged. I came within an ace of saying that. But I didn't. Instead, I became an evil monster and I transposed my manly attitudes into a distaff response. Instantly I knew I had erred. But it was too late. I had said, "Leave the cellar light on."

Which is as good a feminine reply as any female ever made. I was working in the pump room. The pump room light is on a switch in the kitchen. Since I was coming and going by the back cellar bulkhead, she could unwittingly leave me in the dark by toggling the switch. It's lucid, all the way. Even as lucid as "I bought it" when I asked "What is it?" But there is a vast difference. Hers was a natural, uncontrived, distaff reply. Mine was a snide, dirty, tricky, man's retort—unkind and uncalled for.

She said, "What are you trying to do—start something? I asked where you're going!"

I got a few smelts. I was a night or two early. But the first ones are the sweetest, and so are the uses of adversity. It says so right on my star-spangled dish towel from Stratford on Avon.

Ceremonial Ritual

They were telling me about Chime Wescott, who summers over on Harbor Point and goes to Florida, and it seems this winter he went to Florida and made great outcry. Seems he got his boat ready down there, and then something happened within his charmed circle of special friends, and there wasn't anybody to go fishing with him. He didn't like to go alone, so he didn't go, and after he sent out a call for all good men and true to come to his aid nobody came. My thinking is that you don't need to go to Florida for that.

It was soon after that the weather softened for the February approach to March, and I tapped my maple tree in the ceremonial ritual of retirement. We used to tap a lot of maples and make syrup, but now I just step out and tap one to preserve the tradition. Give me a pleasant day with the sun high enough to wilt the snow on top, a day that means the woods are just about to start getting ready to start. I got down my old—now antique—snowshoes, put a bit and a bitstock in a basket, blew through the hole of my one spile to clear the cobwebs of desuetude, and off I went. Perfectly happy to be alone. Fact is, I don't have a sugar maple here at my retreat of idleness, so I have to make do with a red maple. A red maple runs sap all right, and a lot of it, but the sap doesn't have much sugar in it. But since I'm not going to make any syrup anyway, what of that? I told you this was a ceremonial ritual.

So I was at a distance from anywhere, busy at nothing at all, but cheerful, when a hounddog went by me with a deep-throated hello-o-o-o-o, you-u-u-u-u, and giving the impression he had just put up the money for a large mortgage on the property. He was throwing snow into the treetops and adjacent atmosphere, his tongue hanging down so he kept tripping on it, and great slathers of lather dripping from his flanks like spume in a tail-race. In all life's spectacles, there is none with more applied earnestness than a hounddog on the spore. If the Congress of the United States would muckle down to business with the same zeal, a session would never last over fifteen minutes. Unfortunately for my analogy, however, this hounddog was on a scent as cold as a leftover flapjack and he was putting on a show completely unjustified by the locality. The rabbits are up over the hill in the back swamp, and none ever comes this way. They know where their food is, and they stay close to it. This hounddog was as fruity as a plum tree, and whatever he thought he was doing had no bearing on the facts of life. Anymore, at least, than did I with my symbolic maple spile and a purpose absurd. "Hello yourself," I said, for I am affable with hounddogs and like to speak to them as often as I can. Pleased at this, he bayed off into the distance.

Shortly a couple of schoolboys making much of a congenial Saturday appeared on snowshoes, and they seemed curious as to why I was tapping a red maple, but they said nothing. I opened our conversation with, "That your dog?"

"Yes," and I felt the boy who said so was reluctant to admit ownership. Some dogs are like that. But I continued, "He was hot after something."

"Sometimes he thinks he's a fox dog," one of the boys said.

"Do you think he was on a fox?"

"No, but *he* may have."

"Will he run a rabbit?"

"No."

"What was he supposed to be on just now?"

"Nothin'."

I have no idea how many times people have asked me why I like to live out in the country, and it is difficult to make an answer in terms of those who ask. Maybe this hounddog will help to explain things. There persists something vital and charming about a dog that runs hellity-poop through the woods in pursuit of his own imagination, and succeeds in dragging along two boys to help him. Since I, boys, and dog were all on similar purposeless errands, I felt there should have been some strangers to our ways on hand to observe and understand. I said to the boys, "How does the gun shoot?" I nodded at the single-shot .22 rifle one of them had under his arm.

The boy looked at the gun and said, "Well, we don't have any bullets."

See?

I stood there looking at the boys, still hearing the industrious hound at a distance, and I thought how easy it would be for us to make this outing useful and productive. I could be tapping a real sugar maple to get some syrup, to make sweets for the family and to put a dollar in the bank. The dog could have been chasing a rabbit. The boys could have had a bullet and taken home dinner. All of which would be rational answers to anybody who might ask—we could have been doing something serious, something humanity would understand. But we weren't—we weren't doing anything. My futile spile was dripping useless sap, the boys had a gun that wouldn't shoot, the dog was chasing an unknown that didn't exist. But it was a lovely day. And if I'd been down in Florida I could have gone fishing with Chime Wescott.

A Great Truth

After Labor Day, when our schools open, one of our better teachers assigns a little nature study. He asks his pupils to go to some quiet spot in the woods and to stand or sit still for a while and then bring in a report on what is seen and heard. The class turns up a great deal to discuss and study, and this makes a wonderful jumping-off for a busy and exciting term. So a couple of years ago there was a stranger in the class—a young lady who had lately moved in "from away." Her daddy was some kind of computer tracker and he got assigned to a project in Maine, coming here from a part of the country where woods and wildlife are not too important. He tried to find a house to rent somewhere near the village, but the best he could find was an old house far out on the end of the Hackett Road. The place was tight and his family was comfortable, and it wasn't so far that he couldn't get to work, but the remote location was at odds with anything his family had known before. This daughter was the route's-end pupil for the school bus.

When the girl came home from school and said the teacher had assigned some woods-watching, her father thought that was a fine idea. He said this teacher must be a good deal more than a run-of-the-mine quality, to come up with such a striking way to awaken interest, and he said he'd like to go out with the daughter and watch with her. So the two of them went out to watch. It was a clear, almost crisp, fall evening with the sun full red in the west and not a breeze stirring. They went out the back door of their barn, crossed the short field to the woodland, and walked in under a great pine tree where the fallen needles silenced their steps as if in the hush of a great cathedral. They adjusted the straps on their binoculars, and sat back to back on a flat rock. The young lady spread a notebook on her knees and made ready to jot down whatever might be unfolded.

Immediately, both of them were corrected as to a great truth. The expression "quiet countryside" is an immense contradiction. Nothing is noisier than a wilderness. Even Times Square, now and then, with thousands of people surging, will subside for a moment into utter silence—but the woods never will. In the stillest of airs the beech leaves will rustle. A brook softly spilling over a mossy rock will roar. If nothing else happens, an acorn will drop and hit Mother Earth like a thousand of brick. A single oak leaf, escaping the parent stem, will crash and bang on limbs all the way to the ground, thumping when it hits. Every moment of wildlife resounds, until a squirrel hiding a beechnut sounds like a freight train crossing a wooden bridge. And this man and his daughter found that out at once. A tiny mouse, with no tail and ears like mains'ls, came from under the rock they were sitting on and looked up at them as if studying strange animals. They focused their glasses on him, and he looked like an elephant. And he sounded like an elephant as he began to come and go, go and come, in the strange business of mice, and thundered his feet on the pine needles. While they were watching the mouse a bluejay walloped into the tree above and rendered the traditional uproar of perdition.

And just now, above this immediate hubbub, the man and his daughter became aware of a distant rhythm, as of footfalls—like the trotting of the two-ten free-for-all at State Fair, or perhaps the Valkyrie clapping spurs to wild steeds in a quick getaway. No doubt every other man, woman, and child in town would have known what was coming, but this man and his daughter were from away. Out of the puckerbrush and into the

Saunders

area under the pine tree came a bull moose, two cow moose, and a calf moose—trotting along in precision, looking neither one way nor t'other, and galloping on across the township in a thundering symphony of might, muscle, and movement. These were the first moose this man and his daughter had ever seen, and they were fourteen sizes bigger than life. Quaking momentarily, but recovering, the man helped the daughter arrange her notes, and then they sat there until the edge of dark—adding some lesser details about a variable hare, two woodpeckers, and a chickadee.

The next day in school the teacher listened to the girl's report, and told the class that moose, spring and fall, tend to follow set trails and live by pattern. The same moose, he said, would likely pass that way night and morning until snow fell, at least for some weeks to come. The girl told this to her father, and he related it at the place where he worked, in consequence of which about twenty-five people were under that pine tree a few nights later to see the moose go by.

What I wanted to tell you about, though, is Joe Thibeault. Joe lives over on the next road, and he likes to take his little .22 rifle in the evening and walk into the woods in search of the contents of a rabbit pie. Most sportsmen like to hunt the bunny with a hound and fetch him with a shotgun, but Joe is a pot hunter and more downright. Joe has woods wisdom. He sneaks around quietly until he locates a bunny, and then he whistles. This causes a bunny to stand up on his hind legs and look all around to see what whistled at him, and a rabbit pie is thus arranged. It works every time. Except this time. Joe sneaked in under a big pine tree, thought he had located a rabbit, and he whistled. Then twenty-five people sitting under the pine tree all whistled back.

Our Best Authority

O ne (or even two) shouldn't suppose that just because
some of us hang around home all winter and shun the
pleasures of sunny climes we don't have our honors and cita-
tions. Of late, my principal philanthropy has been to keep the
taxes from becoming delinquent, and I am happy to see that
my generosity in this direction helps to support a great many
socially prominent people who belong to clubs, entertain, send
their children to private schools, keep a horse (so to speak),
and sometimes winter in The Islands. I do mention this reluc-
tantly, because I believe charity is best when done without hope
of fame or reward. I want to be modest, and at the same time
I am not going to offend the recipients of my lavish bounty by
exposing them. On the other hand, I have just been invited to
have my name included in the next edition of *The National Social
Directory*, and the communication asks about my philanthropies in particular. It also speaks of my dignity. I am dignified.

There are no words to describe my great pride at this recognition. I leaned against my rural mailbox while I opened the
impressive envelope, and I stood there all welled up. The
moment was memorable, for I had just been involved in a perplexing business problem which I handled with dignity. I was
working on my woodpile. There had been a great ash tree behind
the house which had succumbed to a blight that struck our
area. It died standing up, and as it was excellent firewood and
already dry, I put the chainsaw to it to let it fall. It fell, and

then I cut it to stovewood size. Next, I came with my little tractor to bring the wood to the shed, and since the frost had reacted to the warming trend of advancing April, the front wheels of the tractor subsided into the gray-green, greasy, clamflat clay for which our periphery is noted. This sort of thing happens about every April, so I was neither surprised nor amused. A tractor is an interesting machine. It is designed and engineered to remove mountains, but at times it can't get out of its own way. Now my front wheels, down in the schlupp, had trigged the rear, or power, wheels so they turned with peak exuberance but without effect. So I assembled my rubber boots, a long pole, a jack, two good planks, a shovel, and an ax. Using a chunk of my firewood ash, I arranged a fulcrum according to the best instructions of Aristotle, who is still our best authority on kinetics and the quantums, and with the pole I was able to bring one front wheel up from the ooze so it was suspended in the atmosphere and could drip.

I suppose many people of low social status who wish to get into *The National Social Directory* will want to know what I did next. I recognized that I had two courses of action open to me. I could hold down on the pole with my hands and reach over with one foot to push the plank under the wheel, primus. Or, secundus, I could stand on the pole and fit the plank with my hands. Either way calls for extreme social grace and a good deal of dignity. I fitted with my foot, and then I went around and did the same thing on the other side, with the other wheel. Now I was dripping as well as the wheels were, but I had achieved my purpose and could drive the tractor away to continue my customary philanthropies. The invitation to appear in *The National Social Directory*, it says, is based on just such accomplishments in the areas of the arts and sciences, business and professions, charitable works, and also on one's dignity and service in the broad fields of human affairs. I learned this as I paused in going by the mailbox with my load of wood to see what the carrier had dropped off. The book is going to list eighteen thousand people just like me who have distinguished

themselves by getting their tractors out of the mud in one way or another. Soaking wet, subdued but triumphant, dripping mud, I hurried to the house to tell my happy helpmeet of the huge honor that had befallen.

And one must not lightly regard such an honor. The pulses of the social graces, throbbing on Madison Avenue, are aware of my efforts, my achievements, my philanthropies, and the thought is awesome. In my cutaway and ascot, my ivory-headed ebony walking stick in one hand, I have been observed by somebody as I mulch my rhubarb in modest dignity. And here I am invited to participate—to list my clubs, my achievements, my academic honors, and, naturally, my philanthropies. And suddenly I realize (and I hadn't really been thinking about it) that I *do* wear my rubber boots with an elegance not found elsewhere in miles around. When my wife (they wish to know her maiden name, and if married before her married names) and I step down to the flats to harvest a few clams, I freely admit we work with a dignity, an aplomb, a grace, a charm, a gentility that certainly is not exceeded in the parlors and sitting rooms of the beau monde. This invitation to appear in *The National Social Directory* could not have gone to a more worthy and likely person.

The invitation asks me to list both my summer and winter addresses and telephone numbers, and I think—with my usual dignified modesty—that this will keep me from subscribing. That, and the request for thirty-five dollars for my personal copy of the directory when it appears. I'm going to apply the same thirty-five dollars to next year's taxes, and refrain from distinguishing publicly between my seasonal whereabouts. I wouldn't want too many socially prominent people stopping by when my wheels are down.

Lots of Them

Two or three times I've had the good luck to be drawn for jury duty, and that helps break up the fearful monotony of a Maine winter. Most people try to get excused from jury duty, but I've always found it an informative experience. After you've had a session with crooks and criminals, and their cousins the judges and lawyers, it's always refreshing to withdraw to the jury room and enjoy the company of honest peers. I recall in particular one lovely grandmother who came down from Buckfield to leaven the sordid that unfolded for us. I'm sure she was tough as nails and knew all the answers to life from away back, but one of the bailiffs had found her a rocking chair and she sat in it during our deliberations, knitting, and looking ten notches sweeter than Whistler's mother. She had a soft voice and much wisdom, and a way of quietly insinuating a deep thought into the drivel coming from the county attorney. She was soon running the show, and I was glad.

After about so much evidence and testimony she would tip forward on her rocker, and with "purl one" in abeyance would slip in a remark that returned everything to sanity. When she tipped back to resume knitting, judgment had been achieved. We all knew how the vote would go. Does anybody know what we crude rural bumpkins in the State of Maine call the lovely wake-robin of spring?

This was a grand jury session, so we jurors heard only the county attorney's side of the matter. Speaking of the wake-robin— it is one of our earlier wildflowers. We have several kinds—purple, white, birthroot, and then the "ill-scented" wake-robin. Of this last, the flower book says, "the flowers have a disagreeable, musty, fetid odour." And they surely do. If an uninformed nature lover, taken by the beauty of the ill-scented wake-robin, carries some home for a bouquet, the house will need airing out in the morning. So in these parts the ill-scented wake-robin is just highfalutin' talk in the nature books—we call the thing a stinking benjamin. Children will carry one to school to get credit in the annual spring wildflower collection contest, but an experienced teacher will not leave one on her desk overnight.

So we were sitting on the grand jury and Mother Up-Country was rocking and knitting, and there came up a curious case. It developed out of a neighborhood squabble up on the fringe of the pulpwood country, and the criminal was an old man who, it was immediately clear, had been the victim of a simple witch hunt. The old duffer had been held in jail, lacking surety, for almost a year while the police and the county attorney tried to decide what to do about him. He stood accused of sundry offenses, but we got the idea his long incarceration was meant to hold things over to help the county attorney in his campaign for reelection. Oh, yes—county attorneys live on indictments. They make a big thing out of how many indictments they get from the grand juries. If the cases are hove out of court later, that doesn't count. So the folks who were complaining about this poor old joker in jail came to a substantial group, and gaining an indictment against him would be just like frosting on a cake. Politics. It was our opinion, almost at once, that this old man was getting the dirty end of a stick, and the county attorney was a bahstid. Under her breath, the little lady in the rocking chair supported this opinion. We had been subjected to The Truth the Whole Truth, and all the truth we needed in five minutes, but the county attorney kept lashing his steeds. His witnesses were all refugees from soap and water, and the testimony ran to yes-he-did and no-he-didn't in a regular Hatfield-McCoy scenario. But the county attorney was out to get his indictment, and he pursued every opportunity. The Rocking-Chair Lady kept whispering a synonym for barn manure. Votes in the pulpwood country and an old man in jail for almost a year.

And then the county attorney slit his own throat in a most happy manner. He brought in his prize witness. He was the original barefoot boy. He had shoes on now, and his straw hat had been left home. He was the kid any right-thinking man would love to take by the hand on a warm evening in late May and go to the brook and cut some alder poles. Strawberries on the hill. A boy who would know where the best blackberries hang, and which backyard has the best Red Astrachan tree. Father of the man stuff. Trailing clouds of glory. Grandmother Rocking-Chair leaned forward. The county attorney said, "Now, young man— you know what the truth is, don't you?"

Grandmother Rocking-Chair whispered what it is that a bull drops.

Grandmother Rocking-Chair also returned to rocking and knitting, and everybody knew how this case was going to come out.

The county attorney said, "And do you know what happens to little boys who tell lies?"

And the county attorney went on, "All right—now, will you tell these good people how you happened to be in the Gunther pasture?"

And the boy said, "I was looking for stinking benjamins."

Oh, what glorious joy to learn that our esteemed county attorney didn't know what a stinking benjamin is! He presumed that this boy was up in the Gunther pasture trying to find somebody who was a member of the Benjamin family! Yes, he did. And he would have cantered away with this misapprehension at a full sweat except that our little lady in the rocker leaned forward and said, "Aw, cut it out! Cut it out!"

The county attorney, a finger up, turned to look at her, but she was looking at the boy.

"And did you find some?" she asked.

The boy brightened up. Her tone of voice was friendly. He said, "Oh, yes—lots of them."

She said, "What did you do with them?"

"Nothin'."

"Didn't you pick some?"

"No—Mom won't let me bring any home."

Thus our prestigious county attorney came to know about stinking benjamins, and on the first ballot we voted "No Bill." But, you know, such is the law that they didn't let the old duffer out to go home right away. Prisoners being held the way he was aren't released until the grand jury "rises." We didn't rise until the end of the week, and they kept the poor man in jail until we did. We'd have risen sooner had we known that, and none of us really had the faintest inkling if he was guilty as charged or not.

In Perfect Focus

Radio, TV, and the newspapers try, but they miss most of what goes on. Well, Herman Butterfield wrote to the postmaster to ask why his mail keeps going astray, and when the postmaster wrote back his letter went astray. Then Barney Bascomb said he wrote a letter to the telephone company to tell them his telephone was out of order, and when the man came to fix it he told Barney to give him a ring next time—it was quicker than a letter. And I went into the hardware store to get part number 0-254-63-C for my belt sander, and the clerk said, "No, I don't have that—but you can use this washer here. It's identical, and costs ten cents less." When Tilly Sanderson gave up her box in the post office, she handed in the key, and then they put the receipt for the key in her box. Another good story everybody missed is about Lennie Totman and how he mailed his dues to the Grange. The next day he got a letter from the Grange secretary that said he had been suspended for nonpayment of dues. But underneath, the secretary had written, "Check just arrived—you've been reinstated." And why don't the papers report on the unemployment program? If it ever works, all the people employed there will be looking for jobs.

All right. Nobody like the president or the governor ever calls me to get advice about perplexing problems, and I sit around all winter ready and willing to help. I don't have much to do until summer warms up, and I might be sparing the White

House and the executive mansion many an absurdity. The curious thing is that somebody like Maurice Cottrell does call me, and makes me feel wanted and useful. Maurice fixes radios and TVs, and lives in a world I know nothing about. He'll crawl into a condenser dragging a piece of wire and come out the other end with the man on Channel 10 in perfect focus and begging for more money. He lifts a cover and looks in at a tangle and nods and says, "The amplification is modulating the CW through the interdirectional resistance and the stabilization coefficient is heating up."

"Good, good!" I say, and I think he's wonderful. I shudder at all the things he knows about that I do not. "I'll just bypass this relay," he says, "and that will be twenty-three-fifty plus tax." So when Maurice called me on the telephone and said, "I need some advice," I was thrilled there was something I must know that he didn't. The president and the governor notwithstanding. I said, "What can I do for you?"

Maurice said, "I got me a whole big bunch of Lombardy popples." Here in Maine we never say poplar.

"You really do need advice," I said pleasantly, and as I suspected he was about to offer me some free popple trees I began thinking through the reasons why I didn't want any.

"Yes," he said. "My wife sent away for a slew of the things, and we thought we'd line them up along the driveway."

"Sound plan!" I said. "You want to borrow my shovel?"

"No. I got shovels. I want to know how long I can leave the things out of water before they die."

"It's worth a try," I said.

"What do you mean?"

"Well, if I had a slew of Lombardy popples I'd be tempted to find out. It's hard to discourage a popple, but if you let them stand in the hot sun a week or two it ought to make you popular in the neighborhood."

"I think they're kind of pretty," Maurice said.

"De gustibus non disputandum," I said.

Maurice said, "What did you say?"

"That's Hindu—means a gusty wind blows hot and cold about popples."

"Eyah," he said.

I said, "What about these popples?"

"Well, when they came I was away, and it said to soak the roots in water and keep them wet until planted, so my wife stuck them in water and they been there about a week."

"It won't hurt 'em any," I said.

Maurice said, "That's a good thing to know—now, can I dry 'em without doing 'em any harm?"

"Why don't you plant them?"

"You ain't been outdoors today. It's snowed a foot and more coming. A good robin snow if robins had legs like shitepokes and stilts besides. Snow in May and planting trees don't go together. So will these trees be all right if I take 'em out of water for a while?"

"I suppose so—but why don't you just leave the things right in the water until the weather clears?"

"Because it's lodge night tonight and I got to take my bath."

Being advisor to the masses is a privilege not lightly to be construed. I asked Maurice why he didn't stand amongst the foliage without disturbing the popples and just take a shower. He said he didn't have a shower head. So with the same high quality I would use with the president and the governor, I told Maurice to shift his popples to the sink, and not to linger too long with his rubber duck. "Use some soap!" I jollied, and things worked out and Maurice went to lodge. A row of popples lined his driveway soon after. Before he hung up, Maurice asked me, "Do you know what the elephant was doing on the turn-pike?"

"No, I don't," I said. "What was the elephant doing on the turnpike?"

Maurice said, "Four miles an hour."

An Old Hand

T he Maine political conventions come along in April, so some
of our quiet time is enriched by the early activities of the
candidates—although I notice a candidate doesn't "announce"
these days. He begins along in, say, December with an attitude
of maybe, and he appoints an exploratory committee that will
feel the pulse of the people, and if this committee can get enough
money to start a respectable campaign, there follows a month in
which the candidate is getting ready to announce. Then one day
he announces that he is going to announce. Meantime, the campaign has been boiling right along, and for my part I'm well
tired of it already. One year we had a candidate who tired me
even before that—he come out with big signs all over the state
that said, "Maine Needs More!"

He never came right out in so many words to tell us what it is
that Maine needs more of, and his campaign was just another
example of the big Madison Avenue blah of the supermarkets—
this toothpaste contains 40 percent more; that laundry soap has
60 percent fewer; a corn oil substitute is 20 percent less. Maine
needs more? Those of us who saw the pie-in-the-sky technique
bud and bloom know how regimented benefits settled into a
routine. There was always something to promise more of for the
young folks, the old folks, the schools, the poor, the highways,
foreign exports. . . . Any promising politician had a promising
proposal. But this was the first time a candidate just promised
more, without saying what he wanted more of. Fill in the blank.

You name it and I'll get it. What Maine needs, and I suppose all the states are in the same mess, is a good deal less of whatever it is. We need every bit as little as the candidates think we need a lot. Maybe even less than that. And fewer. Fewer and not so much, but that isn't progress and it isn't leadership—it's merely a fact. For a long time now we've had altogether too much forward-looking vision and "planning ahead," and just about anybody who came along with a bigger bag of promises was a shoo-in. One thing wrong with Maine today is the poverty among taxpayers who have wasted their substance on things Maine needed a lot more of.

I remember with great warmth the first congressman I met. I was nowhere near voting age, but he nailed down my vote just the same. He came to see my grandfather on a day I was helping Grandfather cultivate tomatoes. This was well before radio and TV, so a congressman had to get out and move around. And this one didn't have an automobile yet, so he came by train and rented a horse and buggy at the livery stable. The supermarket sell was far in the future. Would you believe that in those dark days a congressman made his own decisions and even wrote his own speeches?

Gramps always grew a lot of tomatoes. They sold well off his wagon "up to the city." And when I say I was "helping" him cultivate, I'm being gratuitous. Ol' Tige pulled the one-horse and one-row cultivator, and he'd been taking care of Gramp's tomatoes a good twenty years before I was born. He plodded without stepping on any plants and at the end of the row he would swing wide and start back. With Gramp holding the handles on the cultivator, Ol' Tige would cultivate all day and neither would speak. But when I showed up I had to have something to do, and Gramps would lay a grainbag over Tige's back, for a saddle, and I would ride and "steer." Tige had no bridle, and offered me only his mane to cling to. So there I was that day, helping my grandfather cultivate tomatoes, and we had taken a breather and were sitting on the stone wall under a tree. Ol' Tige was chewing grass, the cultivator tipped on its side so the teeth wouldn't impede his lunch. Across the field, we saw the horse and buggy come into the dooryard, and a man got down to start walking over the knoll and towards us.

As he came, he paused to look at the piece of buckwheat, and at the corner of the orchard he found himself a green apple. By now, Gramps knew who he was, and he was close enough so I could see he was an old hand at green apples. He bit, chewed, and then spewed out the chompings. He got halfway up the corn piece and Gramps called his greeting, "Hi, hi!"

"Good morning, Thomas," the man called back. "You've got a good day for it!"

Abe Lincoln splitting rails and Dan Webster tedding hay. He shook hands with me in all the dignity of ambassadorial protocol, tousled my hair, and said, "Got a good boy there, Thomas!" Then he spanked Ol' Tige on his rump and went around to open Tige's mouth and look at his teeth. The congressman (for it was our congressman) and my grandfather laughed then, because Ol' Tige was something like thirty years old and he had about 40 percent fewer. So the congressman sat on the stone wall with us and he didn't promise us anything. He didn't mention all sorts of good things that he wanted to enact. He pulled a jack-knife from his pocket and cut a shoot from a bush by the wall. He peeled bark from the shoot, bit by bit, as he talked. He asked Gramps about this and that, and then told how he felt. At the end, he snapped his knife shut and stood up. He told Gramps to let him know if there was anything he could do. Then he shook my hand again as if I were a real potentate, and he walked back up to the house and his buggy, switching his whittling stick at daisies as he went. I thought our congressman was an awful nice man.

Maybe that's what we need more of.

No Complaints

It was maybe four or five days after Labor Day that I was that way, and I stopped into the little restaurant at Lincolnville that serves such a good haddock chowder. Making small talk, I asked the man if Maine had enjoyed a good summer season.

"Best I recollect," he said. "Started good and kept right up. Hear this from all up and down the coast. Didn't have that August slump we sometimes get. No complaints at all this year—good summer season!"

"I'm glad," I said.

"Eyah," he said. "Me, too. But you know—all the same, I'm some glad it's ov-vuh."

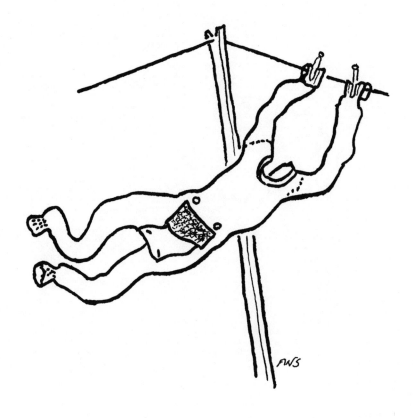